One Hundred Years

The Church of
St. Vincent de Paul
San Francisco, California

1901 – 2001

by

The Reverend John Kevin Ring

St. Vincent de Paul
Patron of our Parish
Pray for Us

Acknowledgements

This is the history of a Parish and of the people and priests whose lives are the history of this Parish of St. Vincent de Paul. To them belongs all the credit for the last one hundred years.

We present in five chapters the parish history as their history under:

> The Pastorate of Father Martin P. Ryan
> The Pastorate of Father James Hayes Long
> The Pastorate of Father Thomas Nicholas O'Kane
> The Pastorate of Monsignor William John Clasby
> The Pastorate of Father John Kevin Ring

At this moment in our parish history, I offer thanks to our Parish Secretary, Kathleen Mulhern, for her assistance and advice and encouragement with the text and for her preparation of the manuscript. I thank our former Secretary, Christine Martino Hein, for typing the text of the Earthquake of '89 and my brother-in-law, Joseph P. Corby, for reformatting the text of the stained glass windows. I am grateful to my brother, the Reverend Vincent D. Ring, for proofreading and enhancing the text. I thank our "Parish Printer," Don Bowcutt, and his graphic designer Margie Bajurin for transforming a lot of pages and pictures into the book you are holding, The History of the Parish of St. Vincent de Paul, San Francisco.

Sincerely in Christ Jesus,

John K. Ring

The Reverend John K. Ring
Pastor

Table of Contents

The Parish is where the Church lives.
Parishes are communities of faith, of action, and of hope.
They are where the Gospel is proclaimed and celebrated
where believers are formed and sent to renew the earth.
Parishes are the home of the Christian community.
They are the heart of our Church.
Parishes are the place where God's people
meet Jesus in Word and in Sacrament
and come in touch with the source of the Church's life.
National Conferences of Catholic Bishops
November 17, 1993

The Parish of St. Vincent de Paul in San Francisco is such a place. For one hundred years now, St. Vincent de Paul's has been a place where people meet Jesus. It has been a place for God and a place for His people. For one hundred years it has verified that there can be no parish without the presence of God and without the presence of His people all interreacting with one another, not as spectators, but as actors in the divine drama of life as they fulfill their rightful responsibilities as followers of Jesus.

This history of the Parish of St. Vincent de Paul attempts to give a glimpse into some of the signs of God's presence and the participation of His people over the last hundred years. It is not an exhaustive or scholarly history. It is a simple attempt to put together some of the documents and records and recollections that are available to us now as we begin a second century. It is the simple story of God and people as the "Church of Cow Hollow," the "Church of the Exposition," the "Church of the Earthquakes," the Church of St. Vincent de Paul.

The Pastorate
of
Father Martin P. Ryan

The Church of Cow Hollow? Many who live elsewhere would have difficulty finding it by that description. And many who live in Cow Hollow today would have difficulty recognizing the area as it was when St. Vincent de Paul was founded in 1901.

The parish is located in the valley between Russian Hill and the Presidio, with the San Francisco Bay as its northern boundary and the top of Pacific Heights to the south. Presently it is a densely developed area of vintage homes and flats and new apartment buildings and small and quaint stores and stunning views of the Golden Gate Bridge and Alcatraz.

When the parish was founded there were only scattered homes and dairy farms, marshes and sand hills and a slough and Washerwoman's Lagoon. The area had been known as Spring Valley, probably because of the numerous springs that ran down from the now Pacific Heights; one of the springs still runs under the parish property. In the 1880s it began to be called "Cow Hollow."

In July 1888, a club was formed by the Democrats of the Forty-First Assembly District; they called themselves "the Roman Guard of Cow Hollow." According to the *Alta* newspaper, some objected; they did not find the name sufficiently dignified. They had only to look around them to see the reason for the name.

There were thirty-eight dairies. The dairymen had all moved from New England, but 30% of them were Swiss-born, 22% Irish, 19% each German and United States-born, 8% French and one lone Swede. They bore names like James Cudworth, Charles Killey, Stephen Tilton, William Haley, Bartholomew and Michael Collins, Thomas Bareilles, David Ring, Jacob Bargmann, and Owen McCooey.

Toward the end of the nineteenth century all of this area, bisected by Presidio Road, was found lacking in good feed and the Board of Health regulations were becoming stricter. More prosperous jobs were beckoning the dairymen, and progress and development began to change Cow Hollow. As William Kostura relates in his article *Cows of Cow Hollow*:

Meanwhile, the face of Cow Hollow was changing. In 1891 James Fair, the silver king and former U.S. senator, purchased dozens of blocks of sand hills and water lots north of Lombard Street and west of Van Ness Avenue. In 1893 he began paying the grading contractors Warren and Malley to push the sand from his sand hills into the bay, greatly increasing the value of the former while creating many blocks of filled land. The expense was enormous, the returns would eventually be fabulous. His property would become the site of the Panama Pacific International Exposition and the Marina district.

It was in this area of closing dairies and filled land the Roman Catholic Church of San Francisco began to see development possibilities and the need for a church. The Episcopal Church had already seen the need and established the Church of St. Mary the Virgin at the corner of Union and Steiner on October 4, 1891.

On August 24, 1901 Father Martin P. Ryan was sent over from neighboring St. Brigid's Church, where he was the Assistant Pastor, to begin planning for what was called a *"succursal parish."* On March 1, 1902 the Archbishop of San Francisco, Patrick William Riordan, canonically appointed Father Ryan as the Pastor of the *"novam ecclesiam,"* the "new church."

It was only at some later time that the church was named after St. Vincent de Paul, a parish priest of Paris known for his work among youth and the poor and the clergy in the 1600s and for founding the Vincentian Order of priests and the Daughters and the Ladies of Charity.

It is also of interest that it was four years later before Father Ryan was officially informed in writing he was the Pastor. The letter of appointment was signed and sent by the Archbishop's secretary, Father John J. Cantwell, on April 7, 1906. Father Ryan later wrote it was because of forgetfulness, but the reason for the delay and for the letter being sent at that time quickly became of no concern.

Only days later, on April 16, 1906, the earth shook and the city burned. It was the great earthquake and fire of 1906. The parish and the people would never be the same.

Father Ryan, of course, knew nothing of the future when he accepted the pastorate. He was born in Limerick, Ireland on May 11, 1862 and educated by the Irish Christian Brothers and the Jesuits. He attended high school at Mount Melleray from 1875 to 1879 and studied at the Jesuit college in Limerick from 1879 to 1881. In 1881, he entered St. Patrick's College in Thurles. He was ordained a priest by Archbishop Croke on June 9, 1889 at the Cathedral in Thurles.

In that same year, in the course of a visit to Ireland, Archbishop Riordan met the young priest and invited him to do his priestly work in San Francisco. He was appointed Assistant Pastor of St. Brigid's in October 1889 to begin a lifetime of work in this one area. His ability to speak some Italian and some Spanish assisted him.

Even after his appointment as Pastor, Father Ryan continued to live at St. Brigid's and it was there he began to write a diary that remains in the parish archives. It is from that diary we learn much of the early history of the parish:

> *A hall was rented at 3120 Fillmore, renovated and fixed up, and, in it on September 22, 1901 the first Mass was celebrated.*

To show the change and growth in the area, he adds:

> *In this same hall the Holy Sacrifice was offered some eight years before, but the place was unable to meet the trifeling (sic) expense attached to such.*

A photograph shows it to be a Union Hall on the second floor over a painting and decorating store at 3116 Fillmore and a laundry office and barber shop offering a shave for 15 cents and a tailor shop next door. Most recently some may have known the site as the Pierce Street Annex.

The diary goes on to tell us that on

> *December 17, 1901 property 137^1/2 on Steiner by 137^1/2 feet on Green was purchased for $10,160 by Mr. Henry Hoffman. The expenses in searching the title etc. made the sum equal $10,200. On that afternoon Mr. Hoffman handed or conveyed the property to the Roman Catholic Archbishop of S.F.*

In the hall at 3120 Fillmore, two Masses, at 8 and 10, were celebrated every Sunday by Father Ryan, who lived at St. Brigid's until March 11, 1902. On this date, with the Archbishop's permission, he went to live at 2174 Green Street.

> *For the first time the Blessed Sacrament was kept in the hall 3220 Fillmore on March 23, 1902 and Benediction was given that evening. Father P. Ryan of Holy Cross Parish officiated.*

The first meeting of the men of the parish was on April 18, 1902. Present were Edward Burns of 2627 Pierce Street, William Byrns of 2411 Webster,

Jeremiah Dineen of 2201 Green, Edward Duffield of 2048 Green, D. Haley and William Haley of 2202 Greenwich, A. D. Keyes of 2619 Divisadero, John Moriarty of 2223 Greenwich, Fritz Klinck of 2439 Greenwich, James Owens of 3014 Pierce, James McNamara of 2474 Broadway, J. Dolan of 2106 Union, James Shevelin of 3118 Scott and the pastor,

> *by whom a financial statement of the parish was made. He also asked the cooperation of those present in the erection of a house and of the foundations, walls, and a temporary roof for the future St. Vincent de Paul Church.*

He was grateful for their promised cooperation because he felt that building would be better than paying $15 a month for rent for the hall and $37.50 a month for the rectory, plus the interest on the $10,000 loan from the Archdiocese for the empty property at Green and Steiner. Those present also approved an architect for the work, Frank Shea, who lived on Green Street between Polk and Van Ness and had been recommended by the Archbishop. Mr. Shea was later to do the Newman Hall in Berkeley and the post-earthquake reconstruction of St. Patrick's Seminary. Thomas B. Goodwin was to be the general contractor.

The June 14, 1902 edition of *The Monitor* carried a drawing and detailed description of the proposed church, with a basement almost entirely above the street line to serve first as a church with a temporary roof and, eventually, as a parochial hall when the roof would be removed and the superstructure added. The exterior design was Northern Italian Romanesque, with

> *lofty wall arcades along the front and graceful campaniles on either side...*

THE CHURCH OF ST. VINCENT DE PAUL.

A 1902 drawing of the proposed church.

4

The interior was to be

> *a fine display of side aisles and nave supported pillars surrounded by arches extending the full depth of the church and around the sanctuary.*

The cost with altar, seating and organ was estimated at $100,000. When the superstructure was eventually added in 1913, this design was not followed.

On June 15, 1902 there was a meeting in the rectory to plan a fair for the fall. It was suggested that it be held in the future church and that building begin as soon as possible. Flynn and Tracey began the grading for the church and house on July 1st. Some of the building costs were $395 to Flynn and Tracey for grading, $5,465 to Wand for concrete, $4,687 to Fennell for bricks, $5,948 to Lynch for woodwork.

> *The fair was begun in the new building on October 4, 1902, lasted three weeks and realized the sum of $11,107.*

The opening address at the Grand Bazaar was given by Mayor Eugene Schmitz. The various booths were chaired by Mrs. M. C. Haley and Mrs. W Haley, Mrs. F. Creele, Mrs. Burns, Misses K. Murphy, K. Hennigan, and K. Flynn, Grace Haley, Mrs. Dolan, Mrs. McNamara, Mrs. Duffield and *"Mrs. Mayor Schmitz."* A newspaper article said that the ladies promise *"no undue importuning on the part of the ticket sellers."* They also promised to have one of the best bands in the City. Perhaps they were promising to have the Mayor's own band.

The spirited life of the parish continued through this time of planning and building and fundraising. The first Baptisms of the new parish were of twins, James and Helen Collins, born August 10, 1901 and baptized September 15, 1901. Most of the early Baptisms are recorded as being celebrated *"in aula"* (in the Hall), but some were held in family homes. The first Baptism in St. Vincent de Paul Church was of James Vincent Edward Trevey on January 4, 1903.

In 1903 the care of the soldiers in the Presidio was entrusted to the priests of St. Vincent de Paul by the Archbishop. In the previous year the first Assistant Pastor was assigned, Father Lawrence Murphy, and in 1905 a second one, Father John Harrington.

In 1904 Father Ryan asked Archbishop Riordan for permission to have another fair. The Coadjutor Archbishop George Montgomery responded.

St. Mary's Cathedral
1100 FRANKLIN STREET
San Francisco, California

Dec. 31,,1904

Rev. M. P. Ryan,

2320 Green St., City.

My dear Father Ryan:-

The Archbishop grants permission for your Fair to be held during the month of September and October 1905, but he wishes to emphasize the fact very forcibly, that in that fair the rules of the Baltimore council must be absolutely observed, and that no liquors of any kind, and no such things as dancing of any shape must be permitted, and furthermore, an abuse that has been creeping in for some time he wants stopped, and that is certain preparatory entertainments for the fair, or after entertainments, in the form of progressive Euchre parties or card playing of some kind, and dancing , and frequently the use of liquor; all these he positively forbids. If there are any such previous entertainments, they must be shorn of the features here named. On this condition he grants permission for the fair.

I have marked in my book May 28th . for your Confirmation. It is just possible that I may have to transfer it one Sunday, to the first Sunday of June, but if so I will let you know.

Yours very truly,

+George Montgomery

The diary shows the fair netted one half of the previous fair.

On April 18, 1906 history was written in San Francisco, but not at St. Vincent de Paul. Despite all the details given in the diary of Father Ryan for previous years, when in high anticipation one turns the diary's page to 1906, one finds a blank page. Sadly for historians, but understandably for someone who underwent the earthquake, Father Ryan was unable to write a word.

The church apparently was still usable. The parish Marriage Register records the marriage of Henry Lowry and Carrie Price two days later on April 20, 1906. There is an interesting note in the margin of the register: *"Had no marriage license."* Quite understandable; City Hall had been destroyed and city officials surely had other priorities.

One source tells us the parish basement was used as a distributing station of food and clothing to victims of the disaster. Many people were camping in the area. According to journalist Frances Moffat, the artesian spring at the Casebolt House on Pierce (currently the Bea House) attracted them. One of the young residents, Charles Gwynn, said they stood in line with buckets to get water at what was called *"the manor house of Cow Hollow."*

One of the survivors, Walter De Vecchi, in his interesting and detailed personal reflections *"My Memoirs of Cow Hollow,"* writes of living in Army tents in the Presidio and then in a classroom at the Spring Valley School (presently Sherman School) and in refugee shacks at Lobos Square (later Funston Field and now Moscone Field). De Vecchi tells us:

> *At Lobos Square the Holy Family Sisters used to come to teach the children catechism and treat them to bread and syrup on a big silver tray. The Sisters later moved to Divisadero and Greenwich where they operated a children's day home. Along with them the Helpers of the Holy Souls kept busy day and night home-nursing the sick and going out to bring supplies and comfort to the destitute.*

Father Ryan and Father Murphy were also kept busy serving the many needs of the people and offering Mass, not only in the church but also in the camps for the earthquake refugees. It is only in the March 1, 1908 entry into Father Ryan's diary that we read:

> *Mass was discontinued in Camps. The few attending being easily able to come to St. Vincent's.*

From May 24 to June 7, 1908 a mission was conducted with great success by Reverend Fathers O'Malley and McKeogh, S. J. from St. Louis. The following year Father Egisto Tozzi was appointed an assistant pastor. Throughout this time, the Sisters of the Holy Family continued to be present to the people. Not only at Lobos Square but also throughout the parish, they served as catechists and home visitors from 1905 to 1924, when the school was opened. They served here again from 1942 until 1979.

The years after the earthquake were spent in providing for the spiritual growth of the people. With the parish's population growth the need to complete the church became more demanding. Newspapers of the time included items on the fundraising activities. In May 1909 newspapers told of an entertainment and social being given at the California Club Hall for the benefit of the church; *"some of the city's most talented vocal and instrumental artists will take part."*

The names of 15 performers are listed as well as those of a committee of 28. *"To liquidate the debt incurred in improvement and additions in the parish,"* a fair was held in September 1909 for two weeks. The reporter commends *"the young women in charge of the booths for their exceptional enthusiasm."* The Announcement Book of the church speaks of a Christmas Festival for the Sunday School in the Parish Hall, sometimes called the Garden Hall.

There was also much talk from the pulpit, still remembered by the old-timers, about pew rent, a form of fundraising at the time by which regular parishioners would pay to occupy a certain pew. One announcement bluntly said:

> *If you did not pay on the way in, pay on the way out.*

In 1911 there was also an installment plan. On many Sundays it was announced:

> *Pew rent for this quarter is now due. Please pay at the church door today or at the Parochial Residence.*

The need to complete the church became more evident. In 1911 there were four Masses. Within a year there had to be five. For Christmas, there were eight Masses: at 5, 6, 7, 8, 9, 10, 11, and 12:15. Children were told to come to Confession at 2:30 in the afternoon

> *...and be not in the way of grown people in the evening.*

On the Fourth Sunday of Advent 1911, people's attention was directed to the picture of the new church. Finally on August 18, 1912 the people were told that:

> *Henceforth and until further notice...Mass will be said in the parochial hall (the entrances to which are on Green). Work on your new church begins tomorrow. Your prayers are earnestly requested for its spiritual success; and for its erection your generous donations.*

The temporary flat roof on the original church was removed and the superstructure of the present church began.

While it was being built, there was a special Mass praying for rain and a special collection on April 13, 1913 for flood and fire victims in Ohio. In encouraging them to be mindful of the power of nature and the needs of others, the pastor reminded the parishioners:

Seven years ago almost today we were sorely in need and help came from all over.

They were told the Easter collection would go to pay the debt for the new church. Some weeks later there was a curt announcement:

Some persons have asked about a bazaar or fair for the new church during the week. You have been told there will be neither a fair or bazaar for such purpose.

Finally Father Ryan was able to announce the new church would be dedicated on October 26, 1913 by His Grace Archbishop Riordan. He acknowledged it would not be large enough for the occasion. On the Sunday before, he announced:

Children are requested not to come to the last Mass next Sunday. I ask you parents to see that this request is carried out. No child under 15 years of age will be allowed to enter. For these children, there will, in the near future, be a special dedication.

After announcing the church would be dedicated by Archbishop Riordan, Father Ryan wrote in the Baptismal Register that it was dedicated by the Auxiliary Bishop, Edward J. Hanna. They both shared in the dedication according to an article in the San Francisco Examiner titled *"St. Vincent's is Dedicated."* In an early inter-faith manner, the subtitle called the church a "temple" – *"Archbishop officiates at First Mass held in new Catholic Temple."* The article reads:

The new Church of St. Vincent de Paul, at Green and Steiner Streets, was dedicated yesterday morning at 11 o'clock. Archbishop Riordan officiated, the Pontifical mass was sung by the Right Rev. Bishop Hanna and the dedication sermon was preached by the Rev. P. A. Foley, rector of St. Raphael's Church, San Rafael.

The new structure is one of the finest specimens of semi-Gothic architecture in San Francisco and is in one of the best neighborhoods. It is finished on the exterior with pressed brick and California redwood, while the interior is completed in oak, the tinting of the walls blending with the color of the wood. The pews of the church are of carved oak, as are the kneeling boards, while the windows are arranged to allow all possible light to enter the building. Light is the dominant note of the interior. By day the church is flooded with light, and during the evening service the opalescent inverted chandeliers throw their radiance against the ceiling, making a mellow glow extremely pleasant.

According to a story related by Monsignor John P. Connolly, who had been in residence at St. Vincent de Paul for 14 years, not everyone was as impressed with the modified Gothic design. On first seeing a drawing of the proposed church, Archbishop Riordan said it looked too much like a pagoda. Father Ryan overlooked the comment. When the Archbishop saw it completed he call it a gem.

The architects, Frank T. Shea and John Lofquist, altered the original design of 1902. On a trip to Europe Father Ryan was impressed by the design of churches in Switzerland and the Scandinavian countries. The architects show this in the projecting, bracketed gambrel roof. Inside, the ceiling of bracketed and trussed dark wood and corbels is similar to European timbered churches. Some say it was designed to look from inside like an inverted boat, which is a symbol of the Church.

The
honor of
your presence is
requested at the Solemn
Dedication of St. Vincent De Paul's Church,
San Francisco, on Sunday, October twenty-sixth
nineteen hundred and thirteen. The Most Reverend
Archbishop P. W. Riordan, D.D. will officiate. Pontifical Mass
will be sung by the Right Reverend Auxiliary Bishop Edward
J. Hanna, D.D. Dedication Sermon will be preached by
Reverend P. A. Foley, Rector St. Rafael's Church, San
Rafael. Solemn Vespers will be at eight
o'clock, that evening. Sermon by the
Reverend M. Connolly, Rector St.
Pauls Church, San Francisco.
Respectfully yours
M. P. Ryan
Rector

Unfortunately, Father Ryan's diary does not include his description of the magnificent church he built. Into it he placed an Allen pipe organ Opus 458 built in 1913 in Hartford, Connecticut. It was used until 1993 when the present Visser Rowland Organ was installed. The lighting was done by D'Arcy Ryan, one of the foremost electrical engineers.

Father Ryan wasted no time before celebrating the Sacraments in the new church. On October 28th, the first baby was baptized there, the child of Michael Barry and Grace Menimen. Appropriately, the baby was named Vincentia de Paul Grace Barry. On November 2nd Father Ryan baptized John Vincent de Paul Connolly, the child of George Connolly and A. G. Gibbons.

The pew rent was again a frequent subject for an announcement on Sundays. Just before the dedication the parishioners were told:

> Pew holders who wish to hold in the new church pews corresponding to those held by them in the basement will call on Father Ryan as soon as possible. Also persons desiring to rent pews are asked to come to the new church and select a pew.

The Sunday after the dedication they were informed of the cost:

> Pews in the center aisle $50 the year or $3 the sitting. In the side aisle $40 for pews of 5 or $2.50 the sitting. Epistle side aisle reserved for children at 9:00 Mass and for sodalities at 8:00.

And a few weeks later they were advised:

> Pew holders are requested to examine their pews Thursday morning and not finding their names thereon will kindly see the pastor.

1914 saw new opportunities and concern for the people. A social group was formed and as the *"St. Vincent de Paul Assembly,"* offered card games for the parishioners on Tuesdays. Parishioners were told:

> Other places of amusement may have an attraction for you, but your own – stand by it, first, last, and all the time.

One week, however, they did put away their cards. They had a lecture instead on the coming Panama Pacific Exposition and the Panama Canal.

But other concerns were on their mind. On the Feast of St. Emydius, August 11th, the Litany of the Saints was recited after the last Mass that:

> …God may protect us from earthquakes and that peace may be given by Him to the nations of Europe.

Not too long after, it was announced that the last Mass would be

...for Peace among warring nations.

World War I had begun.

The poor of the city of San Francisco were also of concern. Archbishop Riordan had asked that, in honor of our Patron Saint, there be a *"banner branch"* of the St. Vincent de Paul Society in the parish. The conference already existed, but it was reorganized with Thomas F. Boyle as President and D. M. Fitzgerald as General Secretary.

Their major event of the year was the blessing of the bronze life-sized statue of St. Vincent de Paul over the middle doorway of the church. Over a hundred members of Parish Conferences from throughout the City gathered on the Feast of St. Vincent de Paul for Mass and breakfast and a meeting, at which Father Ryan spoke of the work of the Parish Conference among the troops at the Presidio. In the afternoon Archbishop Riordan blessed and dedicated the statue while, as the Examiner reported, crowds from all over the city knelt in the street. Present were the leading clergy of San Francisco: Father John J. Cantwell, M. P. Ryan, John Rogers, Peter Flynn, P. Heslin, M. D. Connolly, and J. McCarthy.

The last entry in the parish record for 1914 was the death of Archbishop Riordan on December 27th at 4:00 am.

While the church was being built and the parish was growing in Cow Hollow and Pacific Heights, a whole new part of the parish was being developed. The bay was dredged, sand dunes and marshes were filled, and what had been known as Harbor View and was to become the Marina District was being prepared for the Panama-Pacific International Exposition.

The *"15 Fair,"* as it came to be known, celebrated the rebirth of San Francisco after the earthquake and the opening of the Panama Canal. Though it lasted only 228 days, it left its impact on St. Vincent de Paul Parish. The church became known as *"the Church of the Exposition."* Because of the crowds, the Mass schedule had to be extended to 6:30, 8, 9, 10, 11, and 12:15.

When the Fair closed on December 4, 1915 all the majestic buildings were razed except for the Palace of Fine Arts. It remained, as did the compacted ground that was to prove a shaky foundation for the Marina in coming years.

Financial concerns still troubled the parish. Early in 1916 the financial statement was read at all Masses. A few weeks later it was announced:

During the coming year we will not have a fair, a bazaar, picnic nor anything else of that description. You will not be bothered by tickets at

your doors. We have spoken to you about a Liquidation Society and all who intend becoming members will be asked to pay their first month subscription during the month of April.

The debt was $69,000. Later notes indicate the second Sunday of each month was the time to put their pledge in a special box. They were told:

A list and the amount of all contributions will be published and distributed at the end of the year.

The pew rent continued.

Within the parish a neighborhood spirit developed. As George Moscone, a life-time parishioner, demonstrated in his personal reflections *"Cow Hollow: What Is It — Where Is It,"* those who were born and raised here remember all the names of all the families and all the stores. He wrote of baseball on Funston Field and bocce ball courts and "gangs" that still exist like the *Unknowns* and the *Cow Hollow Boys.* There were train tracks along the Bay and street cars: the 'F' on Chestnut, the 'D' on Greenwich, the 'E' on Union, and the Dinky or "Kilamanjaros" that climbed the hill on Fillmore from Green to Broadway on balanced cables (one car going down pulled the other one up).

The site of the first church on Fillmore was then the Marina Social Club. On Union Street there was Ring's Coal Yard, and just down from the present church Cory's Movie House and Kelley Brothers Grocery Store. George Moscone concluded his reflections by saying, *"Fond, fond memories of times when so many had so little and yet we had so much...Nothing dies that is remembered."*

Father Ryan's dream was to have a parish school at St. Vincent de Paul. In early 1923 Archbishop Edward J. Hanna wrote to the Daughters of Charity at Marillac Seminary in Normandy, Missouri asking them for sisters for the new school. On May 28, 1923 Sister Eugenia Feely, the Visitatrix of the Western Province wrote "regretfully refusing what is very desirable" due to the lack of Sisters. On October 17th Archbishop Hanna wrote to say how indebted he and Father Ryan were for her promising to send Sisters, and he went on to say that they thought she should begin with sending four!

What brought about the change between May and October? Perhaps there was an influx of vocations. Perhaps it was the influence of Father John Rogers, the Pastor of St. Patrick's and a close friend of Father Ryan. He had the Daughters of Charity teaching in his parish school (named St. Vincent's) on Clementina Street. The Sisters in their notes quote him as saying: *"None but the Daughters of Charity to staff it."* And they did.

In July 1924 four Sisters left the city of St. Louis for the City of St. Francis: Sister Isabel McCarthy, the Treasurer of the Order; Sister Barbara Murphy, who was to be the first Principal; Sister Philippa Boudreaux and Sister Winifred Driscoll, who would become the fourth Principal. For four days and three nights the train took them across plains and over mountains to Oakland. The history of the Sisters speaks poetically and warmly of their ferryboat ride and their welcome to San Francisco:

> *Picture the happy group on the open deck of the ferry which, just a little later was crossing the Bay with its bow pointed toward San Francisco. Cornettes waving in the breeze were not unlike the wings of gulls that were hovering around the boat except for their immaculate whiteness.*

> *San Francisco: Yes, they had reached the city where fog moderates summer heat but does not limit the warmth of feeling characteristic of the hearts of its children. Doubly warm was the welcome of the Pastor who stood awaiting the Daughters of St. Vincent, — more than doubly, for this son of Ireland by birth, a native of San Francisco since ordination, was a priest who reverenced all religious but whose love for St. Vincent de Paul caused him to have an extraordinary esteem and admiration for his spiritual daughters. Dignified in his bearing he stood, tall and priestly, smiling a blessing upon "The Pioneers" as he was wont to call them. His fatherly affection caused the newcomers to feel that they were not strangers but simply in a new home. This reverence and affection on the part of the pastor toward the Sisters of Charity, particularly towards those who had the happiness to teach in his school, was manifested throughout his life. He considered the best not too good for the Sisters. If he were sitting in the rear of the church, as he often was, as the Sisters passed him he would stand and doff his berretta, not as a mark of politeness for he did not look towards them; it was a mark of reverence. Father often watched the Sisters as they walked in the school yard among the children. It delighted him to see them there. He reserved for himself the privilege of giving the Sisters Sunday Benediction as long as he was able. After Benediction he would visit with the Sisters limiting himself to this weekly visit unless some unusual occurrence necessitated another. He felt that if he visited oftener he would waste their time.*

Father Ryan had provided well for the Sisters and their students. The cost of the convent and school was $300,000. The Sisters had to live briefly at the

Roman Catholic Orphange until the convent at 2356 Green Street was ready for them to move in on August 15, 1924. The chapel was not finished; Mass was first offered there on September 8th.

St. Vincent de Paul School was formally opened on August 18, 1924 with a High Mass and the Raising of the Flag. There were four Sisters. Sister Isabel had returned to St. Louis, but Sister Josephine Connolly had come over from St. Vincent's on Clementina to be the fourth teacher. Their were six grades and 50 students; by the second week there were 72 students.

The school's mission is etched into the concrete of the school's south facade:

WHERE LOVE OF GOD
AND COUNTRY IS TAUGHT
— FAITH AND MORALS IMBIBED —
AND THE HIGH STANDARDS
OF AMERICAN EDUCATION UPHELD.

Tradition tells us the one who wrote or the one who etched it was not good at grammar. When it was unveiled, it read "Where love of God and Country are taught." Given a second look, the uneven spacing of "is" supports tradition.

In the following year the seventh grade was added, and the eighth grade the next. Interestingly, in that first student body were two future priests. Edward Hartrick Sullivan was a member of the first class to go all the way through the school; he was ordained a Vincentian Priest in 1933. Francis Frugoli graduated in 1928 and was ordained a Jesuit Priest in 1945.

Father Sullivan throughout his life had vivid memories of St. Vincent de Paul, and well he should. In personal correspondence, he says he talked so much one of the sisters used to tape his lips shut, removing it only when he was asked a question or when he went to choir practice. He was also known for his tardiness. One day, noting his late arrival, Father Ryan opened his window and shouted down to him *"what would have happened to Lindbergh if he were late?"*

The Daughters of Charity involved themselves not only in the school but also in teaching Sunday School Classes. Through the impression they made on the children in this program the school quickly grew. In 1928 Sister Mary Michael Ryan became the Principal and she saw the student body reach 300.

During the time of the next Principal, Sister Anne Casey, the Seton Guild (as the mothers' club was called) established a Book Fund. With it the school purchased textbooks and rented them to the students to make Catholic education more affordable. In a few years this plan was adopted by the Archdiocese and made compulsory for all Catholic schools.

On March 6, 1927 Father Ryan celebrated the 25th anniversary of the parish with a Solemn Mass of Thanksgiving. Archbishop Hanna presided, assisted by Monsignors Patrick Ryan as Archpriest and Michael D. Connolly and John Rodgers as Deacons of Honor. Father Ryan was the celebrant, assisted by Fathers William Walsh and Martin Egan. The Masters of Ceremony were Fathers Thomas Millett and William Sullivan.

In the February 26, 1927 issue of *The Monitor*, the editor said there were 500 known Catholic families in the parish and the debt was $125,000. He said Father Ryan could not be expected to pay the debt himself, but

> *five hundred families, by giving two dollars a week each, can wipe out the debt in approximately two and a half years.*

These years saw the founding of the Seton Guild (later called the Parents' Guild) and a Men's Club to replace the old Gentlemen's Sodality. The parish also saw the introduction of the Italian Catholic Federation, a group founded in 1924 in San Francisco to assist people of Italian origin in being active in the Church. A branch was created at St. Vincent de Paul on October 17, 1935. Fifty people were initiated into Branch No. 50 Santo Stefano on that night.

With Father Joseph Galli as Chaplain, Joseph Dal Porto became the first of many presidents over the years to help not only Italian-Americans, but others as well, be close to their parish and their Church.

Father Ryan's interest in the school did not wane. He bought a bus to help the children get to school from the Marina. He wanted to add a business school but was denied permission. He proposed doubling the size of the school.

In 1938 Father Ryan welcomed as Principal one of the founding four sisters, Sister Winifred Driscoll. She served until 1944, an era of change at St. Vincent de Paul and in the world.

Once again there was unrest in the world. Pleas were made to war-clouded Europe. Masses were offered for peace.

The June 3, 1939 edition of *The Monitor* tells of the ordination of eleven priests at St. Mary's Cathedral on June 3rd, and the Fiftieth Anniversary of Ordination on June 9th of Father Martin Ryan at St. Vincent de Paul.

Interestingly, one of the priests ordained on June 3rd was a member of St. Vincent de Paul Parish and was to offer his first Mass here on June 4th. He later became the fourth Pastor of the parish, Father William J. Clasby. And by coincidence, the priest giving the Commentary at the Ordination was to become the third Pastor of the parish, Father Thomas N. O'Kane.

June 9th was Father Ryan's day. He celebrated his Golden Jubilee with a Solemn Mass at 10:30 am on that Friday. Archbishop John J. Mitty presided and preached, assisted by Fathers Richard Ryan, John Butler, Edmond Motterway and Harold Collins. The Golden Jubilarian was assisted by Monsignor Richard Collins, Fathers Thomas Bresnahan, John T. Scanlon, Joseph Renault and James O'Donnell.

The Monitor article gave the details of his life and of the parish. It said when the new church was dedicated in 1913 there were 243 families in the entire parish. In 1939 there were 1783 families. It also had this tribute as the Editorial:

> *Saturday eleven young men become priests of the archdiocese; next Friday Father Martin Ryan celebrates the fiftieth year of his ordination.*
>
> *The young priests will go out to work in a material equipment, which the parochial pioneers like Father Martin Ryan have provided. The young priests will be at grips with a changing America. But the men who prepared the way for them should not be forgotten.*
>
> *We owe men like Father Martin Ryan a great deal. He has been a planner, a forward looker, a practical builder. He has been fifty years a priest and for more than thirty-five he has served the parish of St. Vincent de Paul.*
>
> *He still looks ahead for that parish. He foresees what it will need. He has ambitions for it.*
>
> *On the afternoon that he celebrated the silver jubilee of the succursal parish, he told us much of his story and of his hopes. That telling is some years old, but we remember more of it than he may suspect. It is too long a tale to unfold here, but one thing we would like to bring out.*
>
> *A pioneer pastor is like a pioneer parent. He wants to build a house for his children to live in. He wants to provide them with educational opportunities. He wants them to succeed. Father Martin Ryan is essentially a father. He set out to give these things to his children and he is a success.*
>
> *We make much of the work done by Serra and the early Franciscans, as well we may. Let us not forget what has been done by the pastors of the generation of Father Martin Ryan, who faced sand dunes and build their little cities of God out of the substance of their own rugged individuality.*

They gave all that was in them, and who could ask for more.

All he has ever wanted has been the welfare of his people. He built for them and the light of fatherhood shines in his eyes as he surveys what he achieved.

A great tribute to a priest who served St. Vincent de Paul for forty years as Pastor.

The last child to be baptized by Father Ryan was Stephanie Ann Buttgerbach on July 30, 1939. The second to last Baptism was on July 29th. It was of Ronald Joseph Scola. Years later, after his sad death, his parents set up an endowment fund in his memory to assist the Pastor in helping needy students.

Ill health confined Father's activities the last year. Father Ryan died on May 25, 1941. His body was brought to the church on Tuesday, May 27th and the Office for the Dead was recited that night. The Solemn Mass of Requiem, *Coram Pontifice*, was offered at 10:00 on Wednesday. The celebrant of the Mass was Monsignor James P. Cantwell, assisted by Fathers Thomas Cummins, Thomas Bresnahan, Joseph Renault, and Peter Flynn. The preacher was Monsignor Richard Collins. Father Edgar Boyle and Brother Columban and the Priests Choir were responsible for the music. Archbishop John J. Mitty presided, assisted by Fathers Bartholomew Kevany, Ralph Hunt, and John Ryan, with Monsignor Harold Collins as Master of Ceremonies. In his Eulogy Monsignor Richard Collins said:

> *Father Martin Ryan was a man of honest and rugged sanctity who never failed to tax to the limit his own personal strength and resources to develop the parish given to him in charge. Those whose fortune it was to come close to him realized the depth of his worth and they were unwearying and unfailing in helping him to achieve the end that he finally accomplished.*
>
> *He was not an easy man to approach but once known he never lost a friend. He leaves behind him a beautiful church, convent and priests' residence. His parishioners mourn him as their father and priests mourn him as their brother.*

After the Solemn Blessing by the Archbishop, Father Martin Ryan was laid to rest in Holy Cross Cemetery next to his friend Father John Rogers.

Tall Gaelic crosses mark both their graves.

Father Martin P. Ryan

The Hall at 3120 Fillmore Street where Mass was first celebrated.

St.Vincent de Paul Church and Rectory 1902 – 1912

The Rectory 1902 – 1957

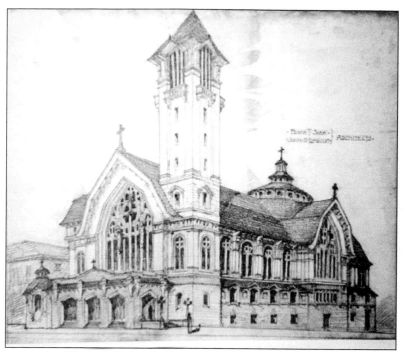

1911 architectural rendering of proposed church.

The church as it appeared 1913 - 1957.

1924 architectural drawing of proposed school.

St. Vincent dePaul Parochial School

The convent 1924 - 1948

Daughter of Charity

The Class of 1931

The Class of 1931

Second and Third Grades, 1926

Girls on the playgrounds of St. Vincent de Paul.

Daughters of Charity

The church entrance 1940

Father Ryan, Archbishop John J. Mitty, Mayor Angelo Rossi

The Golden Jubilee of Father Ryan

Father Martin P. Ryan

The Pastorate

of

Father James Hayes Long

S

t. Vincent de Paul Parish was blessed for forty years with the dedication of one Pastor. Archbishop John J. Mitty was kind to the parishioners and appointed as the new Pastor one whom they knew and loved, Father James Hayes Long, Superintendent of Schools for the Archdiocese of San Francisco. He was on the Board of Diocesan Consultors from 1935 to 1942 and was a member of the Music Commission of the Archdiocese. He had been in residence here since 1930 and, while continuing to be the Superintendent, had been the Administrator since June 18, 1940 due to Father Ryan's health.

Father Long was born in San Francisco on December 9, 1887. He was raised in the then highly Irish South of Market area. The Daughters of Charity taught him at St. Vincent's School at 5th and Clementina, the parish school of St. Patrick's Church. He studied for the Priesthood at St. Patrick's Seminary in Menlo Park and was ordained a Priest at St. Mary's Cathedral by Archbishop Edward J. Hanna on June 20, 1916. Father Long's first assignment as a priest was to All Saints Parish in Hayward. After one year he was transferred to be the Assistant Pastor at St. Vincent de Paul, where he served with Father Ryan from July 21, 1917 to July 18, 1923. After serving at St. Monica's and at the Cathedral, the Archbishop sent him in 1929 to the Catholic University of America in Washington, D.C. to earn his Master's degree in Education.

When he returned, Father Long came back to St. Vincent de Paul in residence and was appointed the Superintendent of Schools. He served in this position for 10 difficult years in which there was great growth and many debts because of the Depression and during which attempts to exempt Catholic secondary and primary schools from taxation were voted down. During the later years the world was moving toward war. He retired as Superintendent of Schools on February 2, 1941 to be the full-time Administrator of St. Vincent de Paul. Archbishop Mitty insisted that he continue to be on the Archdiocesan School Board.

Father Long was installed as Pastor on June 15, 1941 by Monsignor Charles Ramm. It was not long afterward that World War II became a reality for everybody. The responsibility for the Presidio and Fort Winfield Scott was no longer St. Vincent de Paul's. In April, they had been annexed to Star of the Sea Parish.

The war involved everyone. It took the lives of a number of parishioners, including three to whom windows in the church were dedicated: Charles Warren Kendrick, Vincent John Gartland and Frank Kelly, as well as Milton Waters and William Lawrence. One of the windows is dedicated to all the brave dead of the parish who served in World War II.

Priests who were stationed here remember how hospitable Father Long was to many military chaplains who, because of the proximity of the Presidio and Fort Mason and the Port of San Francisco, found themselves in the area. Sometimes he had to put them up in the corridors.

At the same time Father Long was pastoring his people. Naturally his attention turned easily to the school that had quickly grown to 430 students. Along with the Sisters he saw to curriculum development. In addition to regular subjects, it now offered liturgical music taught by the Archdiocesan Director of Music, Father Edgar Boyle. Miss Loretta Hart was in charge of elocution and offered plays by the students for the parish. A Mr. Burke was in charge of the athletic department. Father Long, together with the other priests and sisters, shared in teaching religion.

Growth forced the opening of a second first grade classroom in 1943. In July 1944 there was need for a kindergarten. The only place they could build it, because of space limitations and city restrictions, was in the small courtyard north of the rectory. It was built as a *"temporary classroom"* for $2,500. Although for the last decade of its sixty year history it has served as an office, storage area, thrift shop and now the science center, it is still called the *"old kindergarten room."* 1947 saw development of the school basement into a *"cafeteria with the finest of equipment."*

The year 1947 also saw Father Long involving his successor as Superintendent of Schools in the development of St. Vincent de Paul. He invited Father (later Bishop) James T. O'Dowd to share in studying the parish properties. He needed to enlarge the school. He needed classrooms for the religious education of 200 children attending public and private schools, and meeting rooms for parishioners. He wanted an auditorium and a gymnasium. Together with architects Wilton Smith and John J. Minton, they studied the possibilities. Father O'Dowd wrote this report for Monsignor Patrick Ryan, the Vicar General and Chairman of the Building Committee:

> It is not possible to add a third floor to the present school building. Mr. Smith stated that structurally a third floor could be added but that his application to make such an addition was not approved by the City Building Department and the Fire Marshall's Office. He mentioned that Mr. Minton had taken up the matter with the city officials some years ago when there was need of space for the kindergarten children. The petition was denied and thereafter the structure east of the present school building was erected.
>
> It is not possible to add to the school on its western side since the present classrooms have windows on that side. Unfortunately the present building is not expansible. Hence we must consider a separate unit for the additional classrooms.

Only four additional classrooms were needed for the school. This was determined by the "mortality rate" in the school that Father O'Dowd said was *"a phenomenon not usual in our schools."* He demonstrated it by showing that in June 1947 class size dropped from starting in first grade with 60 to 63 in second, to 56 in third and to 54 in fourth grade. The pattern continued in upper grades with 42 in fifth to 35 in sixth to 31 in seventh and to 28 in eighth grade. What he considered the great transiency in the area made him predict a future enrollment between 400 and 450. If the pattern were to change, he said, more property would have to be purchased for more classrooms or perhaps a new primary department.

A study was done of various plot plans. The best of these plans necessitated the demolition of an apartment building at Green and Pierce and moving the convent from 2356 Green to 2810 Pierce Street.

With preliminary plans approved, the parish began its fundraising stage under the chairmanship of Mr. Nathan L. Bourgeault. Father Long was the honorary chairman and Fathers Clyde Tillman, John P. Connolly and Robert Hayburn served as honorary vice-chairmen. There were 144 parishioners on a central committee and another 190 divided into committees for four districts of the parish. A brochure sent to all the parish happily announced that the previous debt had been liquidated a few years before, and they had been able to set aside some money so this project could begin at the earliest convenient time. The parishioners were reminded that the appeal for funds was the first extraordinary request in behalf of the parish in 21 years. They were told the committee members would be visiting their homes to explain the project and receive their generous response.

The drive covered half the expenses incurred. Records show moving the convent by the Hansel Corporation cost $11,195. Barrett and Hilp built the gymnasium and classroom addition for $306,950. Parish offices were also added to the front of the rectory. The work was done by Clyde Construction for $17,365. The year following construction the debt was $165,000.

Work began quickly. On March 10, 1948, after some difficulty over tenants' moving and one neighbor's worry about their plants being injured, the apartment house was cleared and work commenced on the convent basement. On April 1st construction began on the new foundation for the convent. On April 15th the Sisters moved out. From that day until May 8th, the moving of the convent took place. On May 15, 1948 the Daughters of Charity were able to move into their newly located convent.

Barrett and Hilp had already begun to work on the gymnasium/school addition. They worked rapidly.

On Sunday May 1, 1949 Archbishop Mitty came to dedicate the new building. Unfortunately Father Long was unable to be present due to illness. The building consisted of four classrooms to help accommodate the school's 535 students, plus four other rooms for parish meetings and classes for 200 public and private school children coming for religious instruction. The gym was of regulation dimensions, 84 feet by 50 feet, with sufficient free space outside the playing area and balcony stands for 200. When used as an auditorium it had an ample stage and a seating capacity for 900. The parish had a right to be proud.

Father Long's attention was not solely directed to the school. During the years of planning for the new school building, he also busied himself with the other buildings. In 1943 he contracted with Ferdinand Terheyden and Brother to paint the interior and exterior of the church at a cost of $1,885. On October 15, 1944 he wrote to the Building Commission of the Archdiocese to ask approval for the installation of stained glass windows in St. Vincent de Paul Church. They were in the original plans, but financial considerations prevented the project at that time. He said

> *the present amber glass allows a flood of light to penetrate the building making it garish at times. There is practically no color in the building....*

He already had a plan.

The general theme of the windows would be some doctrinal incident in the life of Our Lord. The two transept windows would carry respectively the Crucifixion and the Nativity while the choir panels, facing the Altar, would represent Christ our King. The others would have individual incidents from the Gospels. The four windows over the Sanctuary could carry the four Evangelists with St. Vincent de Paul as patron of the church in the center panel. Each of the windows would also carry a small medallion from the Old Testament symbolic of the event that it prefigured. The whole purpose of the scheme would be educational and illustrative of some dogma that our Lord taught. The addition of the Old Testament medallion would also give more room for the use of color thereby adding great beauty to the window and church.

The plan was carried out with one notable exception: St. Vincent de Paul was moved to the east window, and the center panel quite properly was given to the Risen Christ. The total cost of all the windows was estimated at $30,000. He proposed that the work be done over a period of six years. On January 18, 1945, after receiving pencil sketches of the windows, the Archbishop approved the installation of the windows.

The contract was awarded to Century Stained Glass Studio, located at 157 Fillmore Street in San Francisco. Recommended by Connick of Boston, it had already done the major portion of the windows of the new St. Mary's Church (now the Cathedral of the Annunciation) in Stockton. The studio's designer and craftsman, Carl Huneke (1898-1972), was born in Achim bei Bremen, Germany, where he started his apprenticeship as a stained glass artist at the age of 13. As a young man he emigrated in 1925 to San Francisco, where in his lifetime he created the windows of 70 California churches together with William Steedman, his aide and glazier and glass cutter.

Huneke told a reporter in 1953 it was his love of color that drew him to stained glass. *"No other craft deals in light as brilliant or as elemental...It may seem hard and laborious work to you, but if you love it, as I do, the harder the task is, the better you like it,"* the artist said. His signature can be found in one of the windows. A decade later, after a renovation of the vestibule, he also did the entrance doors. He said the work demanded special care, *"no tricks,"* because people would be so close to them. A check for $6,600. was issued to Century Stained Glass in 1961 *"for stained glass panels."* In his later years he pioneered in faceted glass at St. Stephen's in San Francisco, the parish he lived in at the time of his death.

The first window installed was Christ the King in the choir loft. The studio name is printed there. The last windows done were the saints, the Doctors of the Church, called such because they are acknowledged as the greatest of the teachers and preachers of the Faith. It is in one of these windows, that of St. Teresa of Avila, where we find the signature of Carl Huneke and the date 1948. Among these windows were ones honoring the co-patrons of the Church of San Francisco, St. Francis of Assisi and St. Patrick. These were once in the church but were moved to the Baptistery during a remodeling in the late 1950s.

According to the contract signed in November 1944, the cost of the Christ the King window was $5,000 plus $300 for outside protective plate glass. The cost in July 1945 for the Nativity and Crucifixion windows was $5,375 each plus $325 for protective glass and $300 for scaffolding.

Father Long is credited with doing the Biblical research for all the windows in order to match the New Testament scene with an Old Testament reference or prefiguring. Assisting him in this work were two priests stationed with him, Father Clyde Tillman and Father John P. Connolly, and a priest who studied with them in Rome, Father Francis Rielly.

The windows are given in memory of the living and the dead. Beginning in the Baptistry and going up the west wall, around the sanctuary and back to the east wall, they are:

The lower windows:	In Memory of:
St. Patrick	Patrick and Ellen Kenny
St. Francis	Virgil John Oliva
St. Ambrose	Joseph & Marianne Puccinelli
St. Augustine	Michael Gnecco and
	Charles & Elizabeth Davis
St. Gregory Nazianzen	Mrs. George F. Brown
St. Jerome	Raiche & Riemer Families
St. Ann & Our Blessed Mother	Ladies Sodality

The higher windows:	
Transfiguration	Andrew J. Branagan
Confirmation	Vincent John Gartland
Penance	Brave Dead of Parish of World War II
Baptism	Lieutenant Charles Warren Kendrick
Marriage	Helen O'Neill
Incarnation Windows	Rev. W. Hughes
	Butte Family
	Joseph Hughes
Mother of Divine Grace	Captain George F. Brown

St. Mark with Jeremiah	Anna Felchlin
St. John with Isaiah	Joseph B. Keenan
The Risen Christ with Jonah	Bernard & Mary Keenan
St. Matthew with Ezechial	Carlotta Musto Keenan
St. Luke with Daniel	Jane Moran

The higher windows:

St. Vincent de Paul	Antone Connick
Redemption Windows	Firmin R. Orella
	Joseph & Mathilde Schweitzer
	Frank S. Kelly
Healing of Sick	Frances B. Green
Eucharist	James & Anastasia Gilhuly
Charity	Pietro & Amelia A. Rossi
Church	Lorraine McDonnell
Faith	J. Francis Arrillaga

The lower windows:

St. Joseph & Child Jesus	Ushers Club
St. Teresa of Avila	Gehm Family
St. Athanasius	Antone & Mary Jane Marengo
St. Basil the Great	Domenico Balanesi
St. John Chrysostum	Souls in Purgatory
St. Thomas Aquinas	Joseph Vannoni

In the choir:

Christ the King	Parishioners of St. Vincent de Paul
Fountain of Life	Celestino Repetto
Our Lady of Lourdes	Pestonjee Davar
Sacred Heart	Anna Armanini & Edith Sangiacomo
St. Catherine of Siena	Benedict & Catherine Vernazza
St. James	Catherine & James Davar

In the sacristy:

St. Peter
St. Paul
Our Lady of the Clergy
Christ the Priest

The stained glass windows in the sacristy are dedicated to all the priests who have served the people of St. Vincent de Paul over its history.

Over the 1940s the people and priests of the parish were involved not only with stained glass and construction, but also with prayer and sacramental life, as well as the many organizations in the parish. In 1950, people could join the St. Vincent de Paul Conference, the Children of Mary, the Seton Guild, the Men's

Club, the Holy Name Society, the Ushers Club, the Vincentian Club for high school students, the Chi Rho Club for those above college age, the Italian Catholic Federation, the Ryan Club for social activities, a folk dancing group, and a Dramatic Club for men and women which offered, among other events, a lively Gay Nineties Review on January 27 and 28, 1950.

Father Long's declining health over the years led him to add a third floor to the rectory as a place to stay when he would have to retire. It was completed by Clyde Construction in July 1949 for $17,385.

The time came in 1951. On January 6, 1951 he wrote to Archbishop Mitty saying he wished to resign the parish effective January 17th. On the following Sunday his good friend Father John P. Connolly, who was in residence in the parish, made this announcement at the Masses.

> *We have an announcement to make which will sadden you, the good parishioners of St. Vincent de Paul parish. Your pastor, Father Long, has been in ill health these past few years. He has reached the decision that his physical condition does not permit him to do all that he feels a pastor is obliged to do for his people. Therefore, he has offered his resignation as your pastor to the Most Reverend Archbishop. His resignation was a complete surprise to the Archbishop, who accepted it with reluctance and only when he understood that Father Long was convinced that he was doing the Will of God.*
>
> *We are pleased to announce that the Most Reverend Archbishop has appointed as the new pastor of your parish Father Thomas N. O'Kane, who has been pastor of St. Rita's parish in Fairfax for the past few years. Father O'Kane will be installed as pastor of this parish at the 12:15 o'clock Mass next Sunday. You are invited to be present at this Installation ceremony.*
>
> *Father Long has requested, in fact insisted, that we say as little as possible this morning in reference to himself. So, in obedience to his humility we shall say but little, though we pray that you may read between the lines all we would say, if we were permitted and were able.*
>
> *Father Long has spent most of the years of his priesthood in this parish, and for the past ten years he has been your pastor. Most of you have come to know him well. You know what kind of priest he is and always has been. No one need tell you.*

As your pastor he has fulfilled, with God's help, many of his dreams. He has loved the beauty of the house of the Lord, and he has always kept it as it should be kept. He has also beautified it with the artistic stained-glass windows that tell the story of his Faith, which is also your heritage, and which he was bound to teach you and to safeguard in you. He has in recent days put a beautiful carpet at the Lord's feet. He has built: the magnificent auditorium-gymnasium, the splendid addition to the school, the modern cafeteria in the school, an expanded and renovated convent for the good sisters. Only last did he concern himself with necessary work on the rectory, the home of the priests.

But his material accomplishments were only of secondary importance to him. His first love and his greatest concern was your souls. For their purity in the sight of God and their salvation he spent himself. The motive of his priestly life we may put into words. It has been simple and godly: "Give me souls. I care for nothing else." And, thanks be to the good God, his first concern has been Father Long's greatest consolation as a pastor, for this parish has grown wonderfully in spiritual stature under his pastorate.

We know that you will miss him as your pastor, especially those many amongst you who have come to know him well, whether through the years or in a day. He would want only one recompense for the years he has spent for you, that you remember him in your prayers to God.

As for us priests, who have exercised our priesthood under his kind hand, we say only this: we have loved him, and we shall continue to treasure his friendship.

Father began to live in the suite he had prepared and to involve himself in parish work as much as he was able. Juanita Arfsten remembers him saying Mass when able at the side altar of Our Lady or else at an altar in a little room he set up as a chapel in his suite. In September 1957 he received permission to have a Private Oratory there. He continued to baptize on Sundays and also to give instructions to adults before receiving them into the Church.

On August 25, 1960 Father Long died at Notre Dame Hospital on Broadway in San Francisco.

Unfortunately the Pastor, Father O'Kane, was hospitalized and could not be present at the Solemn High Requiem Mass on August 29th. Monsignor John

McGarr was the celebrant with Father Joseph Schwab as deacon and Father Clyde Tillman as subdeacon. Bishop Merlin Guilfoyle presided. The preacher was Father John P. Connolly. In his eulogy he said:

> *Father Long loved this parish, where he had spent most of his priesthood, with all his priestly heart. And he has won a very special place in the hearts of so many of the parishioners of this parish, some who have preceded him in death, many of whom remain, who have come to pay him the deep respect of their love in prayer for his soul in these days. Father Long was a good administrator. Much of what is here is the work of his hand. He was a scholar, a kindly, charitable man, very retiring by nature. His outstanding achievement here was in things spiritual, the main concern of any pastor. In this he was, indeed, the "good pastor." The tales which could be told of his own personal care of the troubled, the sick and the dying are many and beautiful. Father Long had a special affection for the Daughters of Charity and the Sisters of Mercy, perhaps a holy coincidence, since love of God and man and mercy toward every form of suffering were each predominant characteristics of his own soul. It was when Father felt that he could no longer fulfill his duties, especially his spiritual tasks, that he offered his resignation to the Archbishop.*
>
> *For the past nine years he has lived quietly. Prayer and silent suffering have been his daily companions. If ever a good home was made for a retired priest, with every care possible for his comfort attended to, Father O'Kane has given these things to Father Long. This has been a touching example of brotherly love of one priest for another. Yesterday I visited Father O'Kane in the hospital. It hurts him deeply not to be here for Father Long's funeral Mass. Very simply and so very sincerely he asked me to tell you that he admired Father Long, that he loved him, that he respected him...*
>
> *The pains of Father's long, silent sufferings these past nine and more years were as rungs on a ladder he climbed to heroic heights. For those who rebel suffering is a cauldron. For those who accept it in Christian resignation it is a crucible of love. It was into such a crucible that the precious gold of Father Long's beautiful priestly life was cast. In it the last vestiges of dross were separated and thrown away, leaving*

only pure gold at the end, the pure gold of a priest of God in all its intended splendour.

Father often said that his one wish at the end would be the hand of a fellow priest. God granted his wish. He has only one further request, which it is your power to grant. It is that same favour which Monica begged of her son, Augustine, when she lay on her deathbed at Ostia, eternal Rome's port to the world: "Lay this body anywhere, let not the care of it trouble you at all. This only, I ask, that you remember me at the Lord's altar, wherever you be.

Father James Long, like Father Martin Ryan before him, was buried in Holy Cross Cemetery in Colma.

Father James Hayes Long

Sisters' House and School 1940

Convent being moved to Pierce Street 1948

New addition to School 1948

New Gymnasium 1948

Daughters of Charity

Daughters of Charity

Parish Meeting

Luncheon and Fashion Show

Luncheon and Fashion Show

Toy Booth, Parish Bazaar

Fish Pond Booth, Parish Bazaar

Cake Booth, Parish Bazaar

Soft Drinks Booth, Parish Bazaar

Women of the Parish

The Pastorate
of
Father Thomas Nicholas O'Kane

B y this time Father Thomas Nicholas O'Kane had already been the Pastor for nine years. He was born here in San Francisco on October 1, 1902 and baptized at the then St. Rose Church. He had an abiding and strong affection for the only parish he knew before his ordination, Mission Dolores, where he went to school. He studied for the priesthood at St. Edward's and St. Patrick's Seminaries in Menlo Park. He was ordained a priest at the early age of 23 in St. Mary's Cathedral, by Archbishop Edward J. Hanna, on June 11, 1926. He was regarded as a scholar and had an extraordinary talent with pen and voice and was one of the outstanding preachers in the Archdiocese.

Father O'Kane began his priestly work as an Assistant Pastor at Sacred Heart Parish in San Jose and then at St. Rose in Santa Rosa. After serving as a Professor for a year at St. Joseph's Seminary in Mountain View, he was sent for further studies to the Catholic University of America in Washington, D.C. Then, in preparation for teaching public speaking, he went to Columbia University where he reported in a letter to Archbishop Mitty he learned more about educational methods than speech.

Although given the opportunity to receive a doctorate, he returned to be a professor at St. Joseph's from 1935 to 1940, and in November 1941 came to St. Vincent de Paul. He was an Assistant Pastor here until June 1943, when he went in the same position to St. Anselm's in San Anselmo. He was Administrator at Holy Ghost in Centerville from January 1946 to January 1949. He then served as Pastor for the first time at St. Rita's in Fairfax. He was a member of the Archdiocesan School Board and was known nationally for a series of addresses he gave on the Catholic Hour.

Following the resignation of Father Long on January 6, 1951, Father O'Kane was appointed the Pastor of St. Vincent de Paul on January 12, 1951. The appointment was effective January 17th. On Sunday January 21st, Father O'Kane was installed as Pastor by Monsignor Harold E. Collins, who gave as his position *"Director of Public Relations."*

Father O'Kane had scarcely finished taking the *Oath Against Modernism* when he was fully involved as the Pastor. The school population had risen to 600 students. There were many issues to study and to resolve. And on a broader base, he found himself politically at the beginning of a new fight to repeal the taxation of private, non-profit secondary and elementary schools in California, the only state to tax them. In 1933, the attempt to repeal it ended in failure. In the spring of 1951 the State Legislature granted an exemption from taxation with an Assembly vote of 75-0 and a Senate vote of 33-3.

On May 5th Governor Earl Warren signed the bill – and then the fight began. The California Tax Payers Alliance, which had been active in 1933, came back to life and sought signatures for a referendum. They won. The exemption of these schools from taxation became Proposition 3 for 1952. It was a bitter fight, often anti-Catholic. One Protestant defender of the exemption said that those who opposed it were like the Ku Klux Klan but not as generous, because for a donation to the Ku Klux Klan you at least received *"a membership card, a few passwords and a uniform made out of a bedsheet."* Cogent articles and pulpit announcements, as well as Father O'Kane's oratorical skills, along with many others throughout the state helped to bring tax-exemption of private, non-profit schools to a narrow victory of 50.81% to 49.19%.

Other problems that faced him as Pastor were not as important but, although humorous, were nevertheless troubling. During his first year there was a bazaar. At its conclusion he received this unsigned message on a one-cent postcard.

> *Dear Father O'Kane – We cannot get over your bazaar where <u>not one</u> thing could be purchased even by a child!!*
>
> *Surely, such corrupt gambling cannot be pleasing to God or State!*
>
> *Do attend the next bazaar of St. Mary the Virgin and compare their Christian efforts with your vile ones.*

Around that time, there was a written complaint made by a Public Health nurse who reported to her superiors that at St. Vincent de Paul School

> *the sewage system is inadequate and often out of order especially where it concerns the drainage of the yards – there is no heat in the entire school; with the coming of chilly weather the children will again come down with all the ills incident to being chilled all day. This is a parochial school and*

plenty of money comes in, but this past vacation period the CHURCH was remodeled but absolutely nothing was done for the school, although this complaint was put in long before the vacation season and our district inspector of that time knew of the complaint and contacted the school principal and had his promise that things would be corrected during the vacation season.

A wiser and more diplomatic supervisor investigated and reported:

The 'sewage system' mentioned in the complaint seems to involve a drinking fountain which is periodically out of order and the leakage drains to a floor drain in the yard. There are two of these drains but they are sometimes stopped up with sand and a small puddle results.

I could find no foundation for the 'no heat' complaint, as in the primary class room in which I waited while Sister Emily was notified of my call, I had to loosen my coat as it seemed quite warm in that room. Sister Emily further stated that although there were furnaces in each of the buildings, there was a day not long ago on which they were all turned off so repairs could be made.

As to the financial status of the church and school and how their funds are apportioned, is no concern of the Department of Health and therefore requires no comment.

To this the supervisor added a delightful footnote which puts the complaints into proper perspective:

Note: Some months ago there was a complaint registered with this department that the Sisters were in the habit of eating their lunch on the roof of the school in hot weather and on one occasion a paper napkin flew away and although the Sister tried to catch it, it drifted down in one of the neighbor's yards. The complaint stated that the Sisters 'were throwing refuse over the fence.'

In the meantime, the parish was involved in other activities. In 1951, they celebrated the Golden Jubilee of the founding of the parish. Father O'Kane wanted to celebrate it in October, but the Archbishop was not available. The closest date was chosen. On August 26, 1951 there was a Mass at 12:00 followed by a reception. Archbishop Mitty presided; assisting him were two former priests of the parish, Father Bartholomew Kevany and Father Peter Flynn. Father Nicholas Connolly was the Assistant Priest and Father William Kitchen the Master of

Ceremonies for the Archbishop. Father O'Kane was the Celebrant of the Mass, with Father Robert Hayburn as Deacon and Father Clyde Tillman the Subdeacon. Father John Connolly was the Master of Ceremonies at the altar. Father John Lally preached.

The growth of the parish and the school was of great concern to Father O'Kane. Because of the increasing number of students and thankfully also of Sisters, more living quarters were needed. In 1952, he paid $25,000 to purchase flats contiguous to the convent on the north. $12,000 was spent to connect this building to the original convent on both levels. Between the two structures there were 28 rooms; 14 were bedrooms for the 11 nuns with whom the parish was then blessed. Father O'Kane expressed the wish someday to move the Sisters to another piece of property on this site to have more playground and parking. There was even a proposal to build a three-floor garage on the site to accommodate 75 automobiles.

In 1955 the parish bought 2943-47 Steiner Street for $21,019 from Mary B. Carroll. This gave the parish two frontages on Steiner because in 1930 Father Ryan spent $6,000 purchasing a house immediately adjacent to the north side of the church at 2929 Steiner Street. This became one potential site for a new convent. Another one was the south side of Green Street. The parish purchased two structures there. It also had the option to buy the Hale Mansion on Vallejo Street immediately behind the property on Green. An engineering study showed a 35° slope between the properties, eliminating that plan and allowing for the sale of those structures later on.

To accommodate crowds of over 4,000 at Mass, the parish hall on Steiner Street was converted into a chapel in 1953. Vincent Raney was the architect and Maloney and O'Hare were the general contractors, with the work done by Fink & Schindler. Between the upper and lower churches there were ten Masses every Sunday, some of them simultaneously so one sermon would be broadcast from the upper church to the chapel and the priests would be running up and down stairs for the slightly staggered times for distribution of Communion. The upper church could seat 680, the chapel 550.

In 1954 Father O'Kane felt forced to discontinue the kindergarten for a year, as he needed the space for other grades. There were not enough classrooms. For the 1954-55 school year there were two classes for every grade except for the eighth. In that grade there were 49 students with only Sister Esther as their teacher.

The after-school program of the de Paul Youth Club was also developing in the gymnasium. The Youth Club was organized under the guidance of Angelo Fusco and Joseph L. Alioto. It was open to boys between the ages of 8 and 19 and girls were also permitted to join, having one day a week set aside for their activities. At one point the Boys' Club had 110 members, the Girls' Club had 85 members, and the program for teenagers had 25 meeting at night.

In addition to basketball and volleyball for both boys and girls, a boxing program also developed. The newspaper of the time listed familiar names on the card: Ed Garaventa v. Larry Alioto, Paul Pelosi v. Ronnie Manesco, Richard Taricco v. Richard Bianchini. In a later year, Dan Flanagan was listed as the fight announcer and there were attending physicians. At a Board of Directors meeting of the Fathers' Club, one of the Assistant Pastors said he was against boxing because of moral issues, but he would accept the *"boxing program if proper safety requirements were adhered to and that only the art of defense was taught rather than the aggressiveness of boxing."* The program continued.

Program financing was a concern to some parishioners. One of them, Angelina Alioto, likes to relate that her husband Joseph and other men of the parish knew how to build a gymnasium, but they didn't know how to keep it open. She and other women with her formed the Auxiliary to the de Paul Youth Club on December 14, 1954. The other founding members were Mrs. Louis A. Petri, Mrs. Edmund J. Morrissey, Mrs. John Eidell, Mrs. Francis B. Quinn, Mrs. Marshall P. Madison, Mrs. Parker S. Maddux, Mrs. Covington Janin, and Mrs. J. W. Corbett.

The object of the Auxiliary, according to its original by-laws was *"to organize and foster a program of moral and material assistance to the de Paul Youth Club."* They were to be fund-raisers. In an interview published in the Call-Bulletin, Mrs. Alioto said *"We women are going to stay in the background and have nothing to do with the policies of the club. Our objectives are to help support and maintain the club, pay leadership salaries, give scholarships to promising boys in the organizations, and to pay the dues for those children who can't afford to."* The Auxiliary continues to do this.

In 1957 all the people of St. Vincent de Paul were united in one experience – an earthquake. On Friday, March 22, 1957, after two earlier tremblors, a 5.3 earthquake hit at 11:44am. It was on the San Andreas fault with its epicenter in Daly City. Father William Lowery, an Assistant Pastor here at the time, said he was in his room and was so shaken he did what he shouldn't do. Rather than getting away from windows, he went to his window and looked out. He saw the steeple of the church swaying back and forth. Some of the children in the

55

school said it was as if they were hit by a wave; a group sitting on the benches were all moved to one end of the benches. The church's Announcement Book for that Sunday had this announcement:

> *The priests and Sisters wish the parents of the children in our school to know how proud we are of their children's calmness and faithfulness in the face of Friday's several earthquakes. They proved themselves a credit to their parents and their school. School will open as usual tomorrow morning.*

To this, someone with a more shaky hand added in pencil *"Please God."*

On the following Sunday at the request of the Archbishop it was announced:

> *Recent earthquakes have caused considerable damage to monuments in the older sections of Holy Cross Cemetery in Colma. In most cases, the damage is serious. All plot owners and interested parties are urged to check their monuments and vaults and to notify the cemetery office of their plans for restoring or replacing damaged monuments.*

Although there is no indication there was any interruption of services at St. Vincent de Paul, there was much work to be done to repair and retrofit the church. Consultants were brought in to study the property. Dames & Moore were hired to check the foundations, and a committee was formed to raise money necessary to address all the issues.

The committee had many members. According to literature published at the time:

> *The Executive Committee, under the chairmanship of Robert D. Rossi, to date include: Ray Bacchi, William Basso, Martin Bastiani, Elmer Bricca, M.D., Andrew F. Burke, Albert L. Campodonico, Charles Cara, Edward G. Casisdy, Joseph Christian, Frank Cimino, Harold Corsini, Richard Doyle, John G. Eidell, William G. Fahy, Jr., Howard Finn, Vincent F. Finigan, Sr., Charles L. Giampaoli, Victor Giannini, Leo Girimonte. Charles Kendrick, Edward King, Herman C. Kruse, John J. Lermen, C. H. Luchessa, Richard I. McCarthy, James A. Minenna, George Moscone, E. J. Morrissey, M.D., Dan Murphy, Martin H. O'Brien, Vincent H. O'Donnell, Edward V. O'Gara, D.D.S., Carlo Panattoni, William Raffanti, Thomas C. Ryan, Francis V. Scarpulla, George J. Stempel, Peter I. Tarantino, Ferdinand Terheyden, Remo A. Tocchini, Ernest Vedovi, Fred E. Wissing, Antone Zietich and John A. Zolezzi, D.D.S.*

The Executive Committee formed an important part of the top Campaign Organization, which included:

The Honorable Preston Devine, General Chairman; Robert D. Rossi, Chairman of the Executive Committee; Joseph Alioto, Special Counselor; Kevin Crowley, Chairman of the Auditing Committee; Daniel Flanagan, Chairman of Organization.

Division Directors of Organization: Charles Cara, William G. Fahy, Jr., Carl Friscia, John Jennings, Edward King, Milt Mecchi, J.J. O'Hare, Philip J. Sheridan, J. Francis Shirley.

Group Chairmen: Dr. Elmer Bricca, Victor Giannini, Armand Zirpoli, Edward L. Buckley, E.G. Cassidy, W.G. Regalia, William Brown, Frank Cimino, Emil Monfredini, John S. Howell, David Lombardi, Charles Luchessa, William Fennone, Richard McCarthy, John Moscone, George Moscone, George Del Dotto, William Garvey, Robert Molinari, Procter Flanagan, Louis Brizzolara, Norman Kelly, Dan Murphy, Herbert Buckley, Martin O'Brien, Gerald O'Gara.

The campaign goal was set at $400,000. Of this, $150,000 was for retirement of existing debt. The balance would be for reconstruction work necessitated by the earthquake. It was work recommended as immediately necessary and essential by the engineering firm of A.V. Saph, Jr. and by architects, Schubart and Friedman.

A "Campaign Journal" distributed to all parishioners on October 27, 1957 listed work to be done:

1. The removal of the Spanish tile roof of the church because of its weight and hazardous condition; the installation of a new and lighter roofing material.

2. Steel reinforcement of all trusses supporting the roof, thus insuring firm vertical loadings.

3. Foundation Ties.

4. Repairing and replacing exterior woodwork.

5. Plastering and patching the interior of the church.

6. Painting interior and exterior.

7. New Baptistry and confessionals.

8. New main entrance.

The "new main entrance" entailed removal of the old portico that came out to the sidewalk and enclosed the stairs to the church, sinking a concrete block which, through tension cables to the northern wall kept the Church of St. Vincent de Paul from sliding down the hill and crushing the Church of St. Mary the Virgin, and then building a simpler entrance and Baptistry.

For the campaign there was a *Solicitation Sunday* on November 3, 1957. Four hundred and forty loyal men of the parish gathered in the church to hear God's Word from Bishop Donohoe, the Auxiliary Bishop, and to receive God's blessing in Benediction. They then went forth on a door-to-door solicitation. Parishioners had been asked to stay home until they were visited so workers would not have to return. Half the goal was reached that day and two-thirds of it within weeks. At the campaign conclusion, 2,700 thank-you letters had to be written.

On April 20, 1958 the parishioners were informed the new entrance and facade were approved. They would still be able to celebrate Mass in the upper church on Saturdays and Sundays, but beginning April 28th they would have to use the lower chapel Monday to Friday. On August 17th, in a further plea for donations, they were told

> *nothing is being done except for structural reasons. We are not concerned with embellishments or modernization of our church. It is and has been only a question of safety. With the relieved load of the roof now transferred to new bearings our engineer assures us that St. Vincent de Paul will withstand any earthquake which might demolish one-fifth of our city.*

The August 31st announcement stated

> *with the driving down of the 45 foot steel pilings and the new vertical bearings on our entrance, the immense structural problem which faced us has now been solved. We ask your indulgence and your sufferance and your loyalty as we begin now to re-plaster and paint the interior of our church.*

September 14th announcements spoke also of beginning construction of the new choir loft and Baptistry and four double confessionals. The next mention of construction is on May 3, 1959. Lisa Marie Herbert was the first child baptized at the new font by Father O'Kane.

The late Fifties and early Sixties saw many activities in the parish, such as golf tournaments and Mardi Gras dinner-dances and festivals with dinners prepared by restaurants like Alioto's, Ernie's, Amelio's and Sabella's. One year, to encourage participation they even published on a flier the school's financial statement showing a $37,846.05 deficit. On the spiritual side, people were encouraged to attend daily Mass during Lent before going to work. The encouragement was free coffee and doughnuts afterwards.

Father O'Kane was interested in the increasing inquires of non-Catholics for instructions in the Catholic Faith and concerned about the necessity of having recourse to books on the Index. To be able to do so properly, he therefore wrote to Bishop Hugh Donohoe in January 1962 asking permission *"to read and retain"* books that were on the Index, namely the works of Kierkegaard, Richard Niebuhr, Paul Tillich, and Martin Buber. Permission was granted. He was asked to *"take proper precautions to see that these books do not fall into the hands of unauthorized persons."* Father O'Kane also sought, as he announced from the pulpit, donation of *"precious jewels, gems, or stones"* for a *"Tree of Life"* monstrance being designed by Father John Meehan and made by Dirk Van Erp.

On September 7, 1962 St. Mary's Cathedral was destroyed by fire. On September 8th, all the candelabra and votive stands at St. Vincent de Paul were removed from the upper and lower church. Eventually the parish raised $540,000 to help replace the Cathedral. On November 22, 1963 President Kennedy was assassinated and the church interior and exterior were draped in mourning.

Changes were happening in the world, in the church, and in the parish. The school reached its peak with 643 students in 1959. In 1960 there were 624 in the school and 120 in C.C.D. and a Mass attendance of 4,257. In 1961 there were 597 in the school; by 1966 there were only 430 and in 1968 it was down to 392.

Father O'Kane saw this change happening and gave extensive reasons for it in his 1962 annual report to the Archbishop. He said there were great demographic changes happening in North Beach, and many Italians and Italo-Americans were moving into the Marina but insisting on maintaining their ties with North Beach. Because of the demand, property values in the Marina were

> *inflated beyond all reason (an $8000 five room home built in 1920 is now selling for $50,000 or $60,000). Rents have advanced so high as to be beyond the abilities of most young families ($200 for a two bedroom home), forcing them to Westlake and suburbia in Marin.*

He also noted that Lombard and vicinity was becoming a motel strip, and many of the older mansions of Pacific Heights were becoming guest houses (*"mostly transients"*) or consulates for newer nations.

Parochial planning, his report said, was also hampered by the possible proposals of the State Board of Highway Control for on/off ramps of the Golden Gate Bridge approaches.

1. A sunken highway on Lombard with transverse streets would maintain the unity of the parish.

2. The Blake Tunnel or the Richardson-Greenwich Viaduct would also preserve parochial unity.

3. A fenced freeway along Lombard Street would establish the Marina District as an isolated island destroying the unity of the parish.

He also worried about the U.S. government's future disposition of land at the Presidio and Fort Mason. All these concerns were amplified by the increased need and lack of availability of parking at St. Vincent de Paul.

Changes were also happening in the Church. On January 25, 1959 Pope John XXIII had announced an Ecumenical Council. Father O'Kane and a large percentage of the parishioners were very open to the changes being promoted. Through sermons and missions and the parish library, people were being prepared in the parish as the bishops and theologians were preparing in Rome. To coincide with the solemn opening of the Second Vatican Council in Rome on October 10, 1962, at St. Vincent de Paul at midnight there was a Solemn Votive Mass of the Holy Spirit which was

Well attended. Many communions. Wide and profound interest of the laity.

On October 11th St. Joseph was proclaimed the Patron of the Council. At St. Vincent de Paul, the Bible was placed between two lighted candles on St. Joseph's Altar to remind parishioners to pray for the success of the Council.

On June 3, 1962 Pope John XXIII died. The parish and the world put everything on hold. On June 28th Cardinal Montini became Pope Paul VI. Knowing he was of the same mind-set as John XXIII, Father O'Kane activated his planning and that very day signed a contract with the Institute of Lay Theology at the University of San Francisco to hire a Lay Theologian for the parish.

On September 1st he announced the appointment of Mr. Richard Watters. To portray the program goals, they decided he should be called *"the Director of the Parish Lay Apostolate."* Together with his wife, Mae, he sought ways to involve the laity in the work of their Church. On October 10th he sponsored an Awareness Meeting. It was a blustery, cold, windswept, rainswept evening. More than 500 people came. Three hundred signed interest cards. He followed this with a lecture series that acted as a refresher course for Catholics as well as those who were not. To help people preparing for coming liturgical changes, there was a Sunday afternoon liturgical conference attended by 300 people. Part of the afternoon was a *demonstration Mass* offered by the Assistant Pastor, Father Frank Piro. A week later, after two nights of rehearsals, there was a *Dialogue Mass* with the people participating and the priest facing the people. In the coming year there were Inquiry Classes and lectures on Scripture and Liturgy and social justice.

Liturgically the parish was alive and busy. Beginning in March, all Masses in the lower chapel were celebrated with all the new liturgical rites. On the First Sunday of Advent, the liturgical changes went into effect at all Masses. On December 27, 1964 a parish Marian Visiting Program for the Sick began.

On December 31, 1964 Father O'Kane died in the rectory of a heart attack. He was 62.

Parishioners gathering for Mass the next day heard this announcement and tribute:

> *At this beginning of a new year, we must regretfully inform you of the death of your Pastor, Father Thomas O'Kane. Father died yesterday morning of a heart attack. You know with what energy he sought to meet the present changes in the Liturgy and so many of the new ideas abreast in the Church. We pray and hope that his trials will not have been suffered in vain, but that a legacy has been left to his parish by his efforts. He has given way to a new age having done his best to prepare his people for it. We call upon him now to continue his labor of love for this parish. May we in turn reciprocate his kindness by our prayers.*

On January 4, 1965 his Mass of Requiem was celebrated at St. Vincent de Paul by Monsignor John V. Silva of St. Louis Bertrand Church in Oakland. Archbishop Joseph T. McGucken presided. Participating in the Mass were Archbishop Thomas Connolly of Seattle, Bishop Hugh A. Donohoe of Stockton, and Bishop Merlin J. Guilfoyle of San Francisco.

In his eulogy, Monsignor John P. Connolly of St. Anthony's Church in Oakland said:

> *From a purely personal point of view it may be said, with small fear of contradiction, that the more intimately one knew Father O'Kane the more one loved him as a friend. For every time he became upset with you he cried bitter tears. But his affection for you made him be generous to a beautiful fault. One of the finest priestly deeds of Father O'Kane, a thing that beggars right telling, was his well-nigh perfect kindness to his brother-priest, the retired pastor of St. Vincent de Paul parish, Father*

James Long. It was years in the making. The heart of the Priesthood for Father O'Kane was the church and the altar. On his lips from the early morn of ordination to the evening of death were the words of Holy Writ: 'I walk around thy altar, O Lord, that I may declare thy praise and tell of all thy wondrous works. O Lord, I love the abode of thy house and the place of the tabernacle of thy glory.'

These past years have been a long and hard Way of the Cross for Father O'Kane. His last days were the agony of the Cross. We refer to Father's health, which has never been good as long as I can remember and which worsened so very noticeably of late.

A few months ago Father made a retreat at El Retiro. He was aware that the end and the beginning was at hand. In his will written then he penned a few lines we would quote, his last sermon: 'Being conscious of my certainly approaching death...I would I were strong enough to say, 'Lord Jesus, come quickly.' As one of God's singular graces to me I am happy to die owning very little...Fully conscious of my many sins of commission and omission, yet relying upon the amplitude of the kind arms of my dying Lord, I ask Him, who long ago called me to follow Him, to take me with the good thief into His kingdom, where faith gives way to sight, hope to possession and charity alone abides. In that fond hope I close this instrument of my death with the words I have had inscribed on St. Vincent de Paul's requiem chalice: 'Sanctus fortis, sanctus Deus, de profundis oro te, miserere Judex meus, parce mihi, Domine, O sacred omnipotent One, O holy God, out of the depths I cry to Thee; have mercy upon me, my Judge, forgive me, my Lord.' Most earnestly do I request that my people of St. Vincent de Paul remember me in their prayers.

On the death of Father O'Kane, one of the Assistant Pastors, Father James Concannon was appointed Administrator.

Who would the new Pastor be? The founding Pastor Father Ryan had been the Assistant Pastor of St. Brigid's. It was split and he received the western half of the area. The second Pastor, Father Long, was an Assistant Pastor at St. Vincent de Paul and later, after being in residence for years, was the Administrator before becoming Pastor. The third Pastor also had prior ties. He also was an Assistant Pastor here some years before he became the Pastor upon Father Long's retirement.

Father Thomas N. O'Kane

Interior of Church 1950–1960

Five sets of twins, 1953–54 Student Body

Blessing of Bread and Wine 1963

Parish Awareness Meeting

Below and on facing page, Parish Entertainment: Gay Nineties Review 1950

Renovation of Church after 1957 Earthquake

New Baptistry 1957

The Pastorate

of

Monsignor William John Clasby

he fourth Pastor had even closer ties. He was born and raised in the parish. The headline told the story: "Altar Boy Returns as New Pastor." Monsignor William John Clasby was announced as the new Pastor of St. Vincent de Paul on March 3, 1965.

His parents, William and Mary Wilson Clasby, lived at 1835 Green Street when he was born on May 12, 1912. He grew up at 2330 Filbert Street. He remembered his mother bringing food to the newly-arrived Daughters of Charity at their new convent. He was already nearing graduation at St. Brigid's School when the new St. Vincent de Paul School was opened. After graduating from St. Ignatius High School, he started studying for the Priesthood in 1930 at St. Joseph's College in Mountain View and then St. Patrick's Seminary in Menlo Park. The seminary publication *The Patrician* said during his years there he sought to refine his talents as a *"preacher, writer and dramatist that manifested themselves back in his high school and college days."*

He was ordained a Priest by Archbishop John J. Mitty in St. Mary's Cathedral on June 3, 1939. Father Thomas O'Kane was the Narrator of the Ordination Mass. Then, five days before the 50th Anniversary Mass of the Pastor, Father Martin Ryan, Father Clasby offered his First Mass at St. Vincent de Paul on June 4, 1939. Monsignor Thomas F. Millett was the Archpriest, Father Martin Egan was the deacon and Father John Carney the subdeacon. Father Edgar Boyle directed the music. The sermon was preached by Father Richard Hammond, the Professor of Homiletics at the seminary.

His first priestly assignment was as Assistant Pastor of Our Lady of Lourdes in Oakland. He served there from June 21, 1939 to February 9, 1942. When World War II broke out, he enlisted in the U.S. Air Force and was sent to Southern California as Chaplain for the Santa Ana Army Air Base. In his five years there he advanced from Lieutenant to Colonel. He returned to his priestly work in the

Archdiocese in September 1947. After six months at St. Jarlath's Parish in Oakland, military life attracted him again and he re-enlisted in the Air Force, where he served for the next 17 years. During that time, he held various Staff Command positions in Okinawa, the Philippines, Japan, and Alaska. For three years he served as Inspector General of Air Force Chaplains. In addition to giving lectures and retreats around the world during this time, he founded *"Our Lady's Knights of the Skies."* Young fliers offered their newly-won wings to Mary, asking for her intercession on their flights.

He did not lose contact with the Archdiocese during this time. The Archives of the Archdiocese contains nearly monthly letters to Archbishop Joseph T. McGucken detailing his work as a chaplain in many exciting parts of the world.

On March 3, 1965 Archbishop McGucken wrote to the then Monsignor Clasby, calling him home, and appointed him as the fourth Pastor of St. Vincent de Paul. Monsignor arrived back in his boyhood parish on March 11th. On March 21, 1965 the Altar Boy became the Pastor. He was officially installed by Monsignor Harold E. Collins, the Dean of San Francisco.

For almost three months, the parish had only a part-time Pastor because Monsignor was still in the process of returning to civilian life. On May 31, 1965 he wrote this letter to his friends:

> *The composition of this letter is proving most difficult. It forces me to anticipate my retirement from the United States Air Force on 31 May 1965...*
>
> *All the years of wandering as an itinerant clergyman across the Air Force world will end. The circle is complete and 'San Francisco here I come right back where I started from....'*
>
> *This week I am being given a dinner by the local clergy. On Friday, 28 May, the Commander in Chief, PACAF, General Hunter Harris is having a Retirement Ceremony in my honor followed by a reception at the home of our Chief of Staff, Major General Augustus M. Minton.*
>
> *When I protested that I did not want such a unique honor, General Minton informed me 'if you have any complaints, make then on June 1st.'*
>
> *On Sunday, 30 May, I am being given a testimonial dinner by the local military parish and on the 31st, I serve my last day of duty...*

*St. Vincent de Paul extends from Pacific Heights to the Bay and is
adjacent to the Presidio and the Golden Gate Bridge. With approximately
10,000 parishioners, a grammar school, new gymnasium; etc. it requires
a staff of twenty-nine people...*

*In the period of adjustment I must go through, I ask the charity of
your prayers.*

On his return to St. Vincent de Paul after his military retirement, the parish
welcomed him at a reception in the gymnasium on June 6th.

The priests of the parish also had their period of adjustment to go through.
It was not long before they were issued seven sets of *"Standard Operating
Procedures."* They were for parish coverage, meals in the rectory, weekly day
off, personal counseling, telephone coverage, hospital visits, and communion
calls. They covered such details as parish coverage:

*Assigned priests will at all times notify the secretary where they may be
reached in case of emergency*

and for personal counseling:

*Except in emergencies, personal counseling periods will not be scheduled
after 9:30 pm. This insures adequate rest for assigned priests, and
potential danger on the streets to parishioners concerned may be
prevented by this policy.*

During the transition period from Father O'Kane to Monsignor Clasby, the
work of the Director of the Lay Apostolate, Richard Watters, continued. An
Executive Council had been formed and was active when Monsignor was
installed. Its membership consisted of Edward O'Flynn, Daniel Flanagan, Martin
O'Brien, Michael McCarthy, Kevin Crowley, Michael Sanchez and Richard Watters.
They were able to present the new Pastor with a study of the parish characteristics.
It stated St. Vincent de Paul was no longer a residential type of parish because,
it claimed, only 2% of structures within the parish were owner-occupied. This
was due to progressive development of high rise apartment dwellings as well as
the progressive increase of multi-unit dwellings. It stated 62% of parishioners
lived in structures of three units or more. The number of children had dropped.

*Approximately 63% of the parish, either because of age or marital
status, are a contributing factor to the minimal child content of the parish.
High real estate values and cost of rentals is a deterrent to young families.*

The study also stated 48% of the parish was over 50 years old. The age groupings from 18 to 35 approximated 27% of the parish. These were "*single/ unmarrieds with a heavy preponderance of unmarried females in relation to males.*" Forty-three percent of the parish was identified as of Italian stock.

A description and analysis of all the parish organizations was also submitted within the report with comments as to their effectiveness. The report concluded:

> *Because of the heterogeneous complex of the parish, a general lack of parishioner objective, and the parallel operation of parish groups, which tend to disunite rather than contribute to a unified parish effort, the following general recommendations are suggested to unify the lay activity of the parish in pursuance of definitive goals and objectives:*
>
> *1. Continuance of existing Executive Council for Lay Apostolate.*
>
> *2. Establish parish coordinating council composed of representatives of all parish organizations.*

Apparently a more dramatic approach was tried. In the annual report to the Chancery Office, in giving information about new parish organizations, it was written: "*The various organizations of the parish were unified into the Men's Club and the Women's Club of St. Vincent de Paul.*" Apparently they were not happy marriages. In 1968 the same report lists nineteen parish organizations.

In October 1965 the parish published the first issue of the *St. Vincent de Paul Parish News*. It was mailed to each home at the cost of one cent per copy! The first page carried this tribute:

EDITORIAL

Dear Father O'Kane:

I hope our paper meets with your approval. It is an attempt to mirror in miniature the spiritual and corporal works which your preserving zeal, rich learning and thrilling oratory initiated and advanced during your apostolate in St. Vincent de Paul Parish. Your parishioners will not forget your pleasing personality, keen intellect, and priestly dedication as you labored for the sanctification of their souls.

I remain always grateful for your salutory influence as my professor of public speaking during the three years you taught me in the Junior

Seminary. Boys are hero worshippers, and you were worthy of the greatest encomium.

"A Priestly Priest."

Sincerely in Our Lord,
Msgr. William J. Clasby

Articles in the first issue told of the investiture of new altar servers and the festival *Arabian Nights*, with dinners served by Alioto's and Ruggero's and Ernie's, all owned by parishioners.

In the early part of 1966 the dark exterior wood surfaces of the church were refinished with dull shake and rustic finish as well as linseed oil. The work was done by Ferdinand Terheyden and Brothers for the cost of $12,114 including scaffolding.

The latter part of 1966 and 1967 also proved expensive for the parish. To meet city codes, the issue of fire safety had to be addressed in the school and gymnasium. With William H. Ladew as architect, a sprinkler system was devised for the two school buildings and the gym. John E. Kramer was the contractor; the cost was $24,000. The gym offered another challenge. With a view to energy savings, it was built with skylights in the barreled roof. On overcast days the gym was full of light. On sunny days, the gym was full of heat. Not only did humans find it uncomfortable, the wood floor found it intolerable. The result was a $3,675 bill for removing the skylights and covering the openings with new roof. John Kramer then installed new maple flooring, sanded and finished, over the existing flooring for $5,710.

The parish newspaper continued to be published on an irregular schedule. Parish life, however, was regular. Masses were offered. Sermons were preached. The Sisters of the Holy Family were again directing the Confraternity of Christian Doctrine for children attending public and private schools. The Sisters were generous in their service to the Church. When they were attempting to raise funds to build a motherhouse in Mission San Jose, it was noted they were unpaided for 37 of the 51 years they had already worked here.

In the summer months for a couple of years Monsignor Clasby would send a busload of *"Knights of the Altar,"* as Altar Servers were then known, for a two-week encampment at Camp St. Malo in Allenspark, Colorado. He would fly there to join them. The camp was under the direction of his friend Monsignor

Richard Heister. Daily Mass was offered as well as wholesome meals and a commissary *"well-stocked with candy, ice cream and pop as well as those items dear to every boy's heart."*

There were concerns about parking and transportation during those years. 1,200 inquiries were sent to those in the northern part of the parish regarding a free bus service on Sundays. The response was decidedly negative.

Much interest was shown in the parish's many activities during this time, among them the *Views of the Palace* House Tour; the Christian Family Movement; the Inquiry Class, a young adult dialogue with St. Mary the Virgin; a tour to Europe; the San Franciscana Festival; a nike base tour; a parish picnic at Adobe Creek Lodge; the Noches de Fiesta; a Men's Club appearance by Edgar Bergen and Mortimer Snerd; and a lot of sports events in the gym.

In 1968 as well as in 1970, the Air Force Academy Choir visited from Colorado. Under the chairmanship of Mrs. Edmund Morrissey and Mrs. Joseph Presti, the 80 members were housed in the homes of parishioners. They presented a concert on Saturday evening and sang at one of the Sunday Masses. After their second appearance one of the cadets wrote asking Monsignor Clasby for a copy of a moving poem he had incorporated into his sermon; he sent him one entitled *Silver Wings* by a Mrs. Mangan.

Dear God, it seems but yesterday
You gave this boy to me
The one who's many miles away
Whose face I cannot see.
The years have swiftly come and gone
So eager in their stride
To brush me lightly by the way
And take him from my side.
It seems to me he's still a child
So full of boyish glee
But pleadings of a war-torn world
Have forced this man to be
And now, dear God, he's joined the ranks
Of men with silver wings
And soon will search the heavens wide
For peace and finer things

But oh, dear God, if in his flight
He fails to come to me
Please God take over his controls
And chart his course to Thee.

While people were reflecting on such thoughts and associating them with both World Wars and the Korean War and the War in Vietnam, changes were occurring locally. Sister Genevieve was transferred to Montebello and Sister Emily arrived as the new principal, and then Sister Muriel succeeded her. A survey resulted in a decision not to have a festival for at least one year. In its place was introduced a high level drawing offering a trip around the world by air with $2000 for expenses, or a new Cadillac, or $500 per month for 12 months. Through it they hoped to raise $49,000 – the school deficit each year. The committee represented the various organizations of the parish: Al Cremolini, Evelyn Tournahu, Gloria Posner, Liana Figone and Edward Beatson.

In the meantime, although Monsignor continued to appear on television and conduct an introductory class in Latin grammar to help prepare students for high school, he was beginning to experience changes in his health. He wrote to friends that he had

> *picked up a yeast plant infection in Southeast Asia which really tortured my skin: They recently discovered a residual hepatitis, high blood pressure, and chemical diabetes. I am still paying for my last tour of duty in Southeast Asia. I must report regularly to Letterman General Hospital.*

And then he went on to admit in the letter:

> *After the very orderly and exciting life as an Air Force Chaplain, the transition to parish life has not been easy.*

He said to someone else he was too used to giving commands in the military and things would be corrected or changed. In parish life he had to figure out how to do it himself or determine who could do it for him and at what price – a difficult change for him.

One person with whom he shared this information had written to him hoping he was not back as *"low man on the totem pole in a 'Going My Way' situation."* He was not the low man, but there were similar challenges. After one of his bouts with illness he wrote to the parishioners:

77

During the past several weeks representatives of our Parish have surveyed our facilities. Their reports emphasize the need for a Master Plan to insure a program of maintenance or replacement of outlived structures and equipment. Most important is the urgent requirement for parking space, possibly underground. If I could be sure that this considerable expense could be underwritten without too much burden of our people, I would like to attempt a solution to the main deterrent to optimum Mass attendance. With 3,700 families or about 10,000 parishioners, an average congregation of 3,000 per Sunday is most discouraging.

One of the architects consulted stated as his considered opinion that the land upon which our Parish structure is built is too valuable not to have functional structures for maximum use. He proposed a twenty year program of improvement and replacement of buildings which are deteriorating.

In thanking you for your consistent help and support, I request your considered opinions and suggestions for the immediate and future development of our Parish structures.

To the letter he added this:

P.S. Our Sanctuary is no longer functional for the new liturgy. If you study the main altar structure you will note how shabby it is. We must either renovate or reconstruct to meet our needs.

The opinions and suggestions he received must have been to move slowly.

In 1971, the agenda for the Parish Executive Council meeting included items about the removal of church altar rails, replacement of church carpeting, promotional methods to emphasize Monday Novena to Our Lady of Fatima, revival of Benediction of the Blessed Sacrament as a liturgical service. Again the parish must have decided to move slowly.

Tension developed, however, about the slowness or lack of movement. The following year Richard Watters chaired a Steering Committee meeting to address the issue. Present were Bill O'Relli, Dan Flanagan, Ed O'Flynn, Bob Christian, Ron Pimentel, and Marie Gandolfo. No clergy were present. In a frank discussion, there was general acceptance of the Executive Council the Pastor already had. They defined it as being only for policy and for business problems. To get the parish moving, they saw the need for a Coordinating Council, its membership composed of heads of the various parish organizations. It would work without clergy so they could talk freely and not be told what to do. It also called for a complete breakdown of finances. All its ideas were to be shared with the Pastor. They did not think the Coordinating Council or the laity should want to run the parish.

And using the talents and prayers of the priests and laity, the parish continued to run and serve the many needs of the people. There were the First Communions and Confirmations, the Noel Balls and Fashion Shows and Silent Auctions. There were golf tournaments at San Francisco Golf Club arranged by Dr. Edward Morrissey, Lucien Sabella, William Bentley and Lou Menconi, followed by gourmet dinner-dances. There was a performance by Dennis Day at a Men's Club dinner in 1974. He was even offered accommodations in the priest's house, of what Monsignor told him was a *"geriatrics parish consisting of Irish and Italian people."* And there were festivals called *South Pacific Nights, The Roaring 20s* and *Weekend in Italy.* The school and the gym were the beneficiaries of these events.

The 50th anniversary of St. Vincent de Paul School was celebrated in 1975. A Fashion show entitled *"Let's Celebrate 50 Years"* began the year on February 6th. It was offered by the Seton Guild at the St. Francis Yacht Club.

The Golden Jubilee Mass was offered on April 19th. Monsignor Clasby was the Principal Celebrant. Concelebrating with him were Monsignors John P. Connolly, Pierre Du Maine, and Robert Hayburn and Fathers William Lowery, Louis Robello, Charles Muldoon, Lawrence Finegan and James Fox. At the Offertory the Petitions were by Sister Genevieve, DC, Alice Devine, Stephanie Dunne, Anthony Rodgers, and Robert Barbieri: Offering the gifts were Sister Marguerite, DC, Sister Janice, DC, Sister Sylvia, SNJM, Helen Arm and Anne McCaddon. In his sermon, Monsignor Connolly recounted the history of the parish and the school from Sister Barbara, the first principal, to the then principal, Sister Stella Joseph. In praising the Daughters of Charity, he said they were *"like graceful white swans on a beautiful lake on a delightful summer day."*

That year also witnessed refurbishment of the church. Through the generous donation of James Davar, the parish was able to paint the church interior and make other changes. The cost of the project was $115,000. Perhaps it was at this time the slender spires on the old altar were removed so they would not interfere with the view of the Resurrection window. Definitely at this time the walls of the sanctuary were painted blue. One of the parishioners, Elena Madison, said it was to honor the Pastor's Air Force background. She called it *"Fly-into-the-wild-*

blue-yonder" blue. On December 20th Archbishop McGucken came to offer Mass with the priests of the parish and to honor Mr. Davar.

In 1982 the church exterior was painted. Gone was the wood stain. Now it was green and red and white, very pleasing colors to Italians according to the Pastor, as he also pointed out to them green was on the top. To raise money for the work he wrote to the parishioners for what he called a *"Paint Pot emergency."* He told them the bids were from $54,000 to over $80,000 with scaffolding costs of $18,000. He even appealed to Archbishop John R. Quinn, whose residence was in the parish at the time. As a good parishioner the Archbishop did send a donation.

In his letter writing Monsignor Clasby was not afraid to beg for donations for the school. Known for his personal generosity in helping students, he sought the generosity of old friends as well as parishioners, military connections as well as foundations. Very clearly he told them our parochial school system was of benefit to the entire Church. And yet only 300 of the 3,100 parishioners were contributing to the school collection. There was full financial disclosure in regard to the school. Normally it showed tuition was covering less than 50% of expenses. Through church subsidies and special events and his begging, the books were kept in balance.

The parish archives contain not only letters from but also letters to Monsignor Clasby. There are letters from students he helped, from places where he preached or gave retreats, from those with whom he served in younger days. There is even a letter from one of the school students, now a prominent parishioner, telling him all about his first plane ride to Glen Lyon, Pennsylvania and how scary it was. And the student gave the address where he was staying, hoping for a response. He probably got one because Monsignor kept the letter.

Sometimes letters to him did create letters from him offering free advice. Mayor Joseph Alioto, a parishioner, sent a donation from the Mayor's Youth Bowl Fund to the de Paul Youth Club. He was running for Governor. He received this advice:

> *I am prayerfully watching your campaign. Continue to try to create in the public a felt need for what you purpose to accomplish as Governor. Surround yourself with the very best public relations group you can find. Then make them sell, sell, sell. Your opponents cannot match you as a public speaker. It might prove valuable for you to renew the techniques which Aristotle set forth in 'The Rhetoric', to my knowledge the best work ever written on the devices available to a public speaker as he seeks to win an audience to his cause.*

A letter from the National Conference of Bar Examiners seeking his frank opinion concerning a parishioner must have sent them to their dictionary. They were told that

> *I sometimes think she somehow intellectually intussuscepted Aristotle's Rhetoric by osmosis.*

And he was not above pulling rank whenever advantageous. In one case, a graduate of the school ended up in jail. Monsignor wrote to the Judge admitting he had taught the miscreant, seeking probation and promising he would meet with him once a week to insure there was no more foolish behavior. He declared

> *I am writing these lines drawn upon my background of almost twenty-four years as a Chaplain in the United States Air Force, (18 years a Colonel), and in particular as Inspector General for three years in the area of the Chaplains purview and as the Air University Command Chaplain also for three years. I also draw upon my experience as Retreat Master at Father Flanagan's Boys Town over a period of 21 years, and as a member of the Bay Area Social Planning Commission, with the Clasby report on the San Francisco Juvenile Detention Facility as the climax of our study (most of which has been implemented).*

All his history and all his influence could not prevent writing a sad letter to the parishioners on September 12, 1985. He told the history of the school. He praised the 80 Daughters of Charity who taught in the school over the years. Then he had to announce:

> *Now I must write lines that I never thought I would ever have to write. At the end of this school year the Daughters of Charity must withdraw from our Parish school. As you know, for some time we have had only two Sisters assigned to our faculty. This has been due to the lack of vocations.*
>
> *I hasten to assure you that St. Vincent de Paul School will NOT close. We have an outstanding lay faculty and Sister Ange, a most competent BVM Sister, teaching in 6th Grade.*

The principal, Sister Frances Meyer, DC, then wrote to the parents:

> *At the end of the 1985-86 school year we will no longer be on the staff of the school. Our Community has anguished over this decision but had to face the fact that we no longer have the number of Sisters available to*

staff the schools in which we have worked in the past. The number of vocations to the Daughters of Charity have not been such that we can continue to supply Sisters to all the schools.

In looking at the schools in which we were present and rigorously appraising all the circumstances it was decided that we would withdraw from schools that were the most healthy. St. Vincent de Paul has always been considered the "cream of the crop" in our school circles and without a doubt would be the one "most likely to be able to carry on without the Daughters.

On June 1, 1986 the Parish had a Mass and Farewell Reception for the Sisters, sponsored by the Seton Family Guild, the Men's Club, the Alumni, the Swinging 60s, the Auxiliary to the de Paul Youth, and the Italian Catholic Federation. It was chaired by Maryanne Harrison and Sandie Tucker. They honored the last two Sisters, Sister Frances and Sister Madeleine Brennan, DC. A memorial plaque in the main hall of the school was dedicated. It read:

MAY OUR LORD BE
– THE JOY OF YOUR HEART
– THE SOUL OF YOUR ACTIONS
– YOUR GLORY IN HEAVEN
——ST. VINCENT DE PAUL

WITH GRATITUDE AND ADMIRATION
WE HONOR
THE DAUGHTERS OF CHARITY OF ST. VINCENT DE PAUL
FOR
SIX DECADES OF SERVICE TO THE
CHILDREN AND FAMILIES
OF ST. VINCENT DE PAUL PARISH.
1924 – 1986
THEY HAVE ATTAINED THE IDEALS
OF
THEIR FOUNDER

Sister Frances, in her words of thanks and farewell, quoted Flavia: *"Some people come into our lives and quickly go. Some stay for awhile and leave foot prints on our hearts, and we will never, ever be the same."*

Sadly, the search had to begin for a new principal. A Presentation Sister, Sister Ann Conlon, was chosen to carry on the tradition of the Daughters of Charity.

Monsignor did not outlive the Daughters for long. He did witness the opening of the school in the Fall. However, he was diagnosed with liver cancer that was traceable to the hepatitis he contracted in Vietnam thirty years earlier. He died on Monday, November 3, 1986. He was 74.

Monsignor Clasby lay in state in St. Vincent de Paul Church and the Rosary was recited for him on Thursday evening. On Friday, November 7th, his funeral Mass was celebrated at St. Mary's Cathedral. Archbishop John R. Quinn was the Principal Celebrant. Bishop Daniel Walsh, Monsignor Richard Heister, Monsignor James Wilders, Father James L. Spooncer, and Father Cliff Martin were among the concelebrants. Father Michele Raimondi was the Cantor; Rosalie Cirby and George Moscone represented the parish as Lectors.

In his homily, Monsignor Wilders spoke of their ordination on the same day in 1939, one in New York, the other in San Francisco. Although they did not know one another then, he referred to Monsignor Clasby as his closest priest friend for the last forty years. He spoke of the meaning of Priesthood – the Priesthood of Jesus, the Priesthood of William John Clasby. He concluded by asking all to join in

A Prayer for Priests

*Lord Jesus, you have chosen your priests from among us
and sent them out to proclaim your word and to act in
your name. For so great a gift to your church, we give you praise
and thanksgiving.*

*We ask you to fill them with the fire of your love,
that their ministry may reveal your presence in the Church.
Since they are earthen vessels, we pray that your power
shine out through their weakness.
In their affliction, let them never be crushed;
in their doubts, never despair;
in temptation, never be destroyed;
in persecution, never abandoned.*

*Inspire them through prayer to live each day the mystery
of your dying and rising.
In times of weakness, send them your spirit,
and help them to praise your heavenly Father
and pray for poor sinners.*

By the same Holy Spirit, put your word on their lips
and your love in their hearts, to bring good news to the
poor and healing to the broken-hearted.

And may the gift of Mary your mother, to the disciple
whom you loved, be your gift to every priest.
Grant that she who formed you in her human image
may form them in your divine image,
by the power of your Spirit, to the glory of God the Father

Amen.

On May 17, 1987 a memorial plaque was dedicated to the Monsignor in the church, and his successor as Pastor, using as part of the blessing the Latin text inscribed on the marble, said:

Monsignor William John Clasby
Fourth Pastor of St. Vincent de Paul Church
> *who died in the Lord on the 3rd of November 1986*
> *To him we dedicate this plaque*
> *To him who was "Semper fervens in spiritu,*
>> *Gaudens in spe*
>> *Semper tuo nomine serviens*
>>> *Always fervent in spirit*
>>> *Joyful in hope*
>>> *Always serving in your name"*

On this day – as his personal family and his parish family
> *we gather to honor not marble but a man –*
>> *a man whose memory is now carved in marble*
>> *a man whose works and words are etched in our minds*
>> *a man who was a man and a Cow Hollow boy*
>> *a man who traveled the world and never left home*
>> *a man who was a citizen and a colonel, and always*
>>> *a priest and a pastor -*

May all who pause to pray by this plaque we now bless
> *be themselves blessed now and forever.*

The Parish of St. Vincent de Paul was, after 21 years, like *"sheep without a shepherd."* There was no Administrator ready to assume the title of Pastor. There was no former altar boy awaiting an assignment. And now the Archdiocese of San Francisco had a process for the appointment of a Pastor. The Personnel Board of the Archdiocese and the Dean of the area had to meet with the parish staff and then with the people of the parish in an open meeting. They were to listen to the people as they spoke of the qualities and talents they thought necessary in the new Pastor.

The staff and the people of the parish were asked to identify what was happening in the parish that they wished to continue and what dreams they had for the future life of the parish. All the specific comments and observations were written up by the Personnel Board and the Dean, Father James MacDonald, and sent with their summary to Archbishop Quinn for his study and decision. The summary stated that the new Pastor needed to have these skills:

1. He needs to be able to help people feel welcome in their parish.

2. He needs to be able to make difficult decisions and be able to take criticism. (In the words of a parishioner, he needs the ability to laugh at himself when he gets criticized.)

3. He needs to have had administrative experience in finances and plant maintenance.

4. He should be someone committed to quality liturgy and adult religious education.

The Consultation took place on December 2, 1986. All the information gathered plus a demographic study of the parish was presented to the Archbishop.

Monsignor William J. Clasby

The Church in the late 70s

Installation of Monsignor Clasby

Daughters of Charity

Parish event

Holy Thursday Liturgy

Bazaar Committee

Sports Night

Archbishop McGucken at a Parish event

Church interior 1970s

Church interior 1980s

Parish event

Parish event

Parish event

The chefs of St. Vincent de Paul, 1967

Parish entertainment

The Pastorate

of

Father John K. Ring

On December 19, 1986, Archbishop Quinn appointed Father John Kevin Ring as the fifth Pastor of St. Vincent de Paul. He was the Pastor of Mater Dolorosa Church in South San Francisco. Unlike his predecessors, he had no previous connection to St. Vincent de Paul. He was not related to the David Ring who from 1862 to 1865 was a dairyman on Lombard Street, or to the Rings who had a coal yard on Union Street in the 1920s, or to the ones baptized or married here with that name.

He was born in San Francisco on August 13, 1935, the son of John and Mary Murphy Ring. With his sister Patricia and brother Vincent (currently the Pastor of St. Robert's Church in San Bruno) he grew up in St. Anne's Parish in the Sunset. He was baptized, went to school, and received all the Sacraments there. He entered the seminary at St. Joseph's College in Mountain View in 1949 and continued his studies for the Priesthood at St. Patrick's Seminary in Menlo Park. He was ordained a Priest by Bishop Merlin Guilfoyle on June 10, 1961 at St. Mary's Cathedral. The following day, he offered his First Mass at St. Anne's Church. The homily was preached by the Pastor of St. Anne's since before he was born, Monsignor Patrick G. Moriarty. His first cousin from Chicago, Father John D. Ring, was his deacon and his brother Vincent the subdeacon. The Archpriest was the Director of the Confraternity of Christian Doctrine, Monsignor John Scanlon.

Father Ring's first priestly assignment was Most Holy Redeemer Parish in San Francisco with Monsignor Henry J. Lyne. He served there for four years and then spent six years at St. Patrick's in Larkspur, where he also headed the High School of Religion program for all of Marin County. For five years he was the Assistant Pastor at St. Matthew's in San Mateo and then at St. Patrick's again for almost three years. St. Brigid's in San Francisco was his last assignment as Assistant Pastor. He was sent there also to be the Master of Ceremonies for the Pastor, Bishop William McDonald. After three years at St. Brigid's, Archbishop

Quinn made him Pastor of Mater Dolorosa Church on March 24, 1981, where he added on to and remodeled the church. He moved the convent next to the school. He had just completed the celebration of the parish's 25th anniversary, as well as his own Silver Jubilee as a Priest, when Archbishop Quinn appointed him Pastor of St. Vincent de Paul.

Father Ring arrived at St. Vincent de Paul on January 26, 1987. Archbishop Quinn himself came to install him as Pastor on February 8, 1987. The people of the parish welcomed him at a Reception after the Mass in the gymnasium.

The parish put him to work immediately. A parishioner who was also an architect introduced himself at the reception and said he wanted to help in the work that needed to be done. Father Ring called Steven Semes the next day, met with him and asked him to study the parish properties and make recommendations. He thus began to address one of the primary concerns identified in the Parish Consultation.

What was said in that consultation he wanted to hear with his own ears as well. He told the people he wanted them to teach him how to be a Pastor for them. He announced there would be *"Listening and Learning Sessions."* The first one on February 17th was to be on *"The Parish as a Worshipping Community."* The second one on the following Tuesday was on *"The Parish as an Evangelizing Community."* The final one on March 3rd addressed *"The Parish as a Serving Community."* There was a beneficial sharing of ideas at these sessions. For the sake of those who found it impossible to be present, a survey was also printed in the bulletin, through which people could share their ideas.

Through these exchanges Father Ring learned that, for the sake of parish unity, he would have to move slower in some of the ideas he wished to foster. And the parishioners learned that, for the sake of conformity with the Church, with some ideas the pace would have to move a little faster. Because of the sessions and the survey and the consultation, he was able to prioritize and set his agenda for the year. In a presentation to the parish he was able to list his priorities:

1. to offer Liturgies that are beautiful and prayerful with full involvement of the laity and seven-minute homilies by the clergy and quality music.

2. to insure the survival of the school by stabilizing its finances through an increase in tuition and a decrease in subsidy.

3. to involve the laity in all the ministries of the Church particularly for the young and the sick and the needy.

4. to care for the property.

To address the first priorities, the parish was most fortunate to have hired for the Installation Mass a core group of singers to help with the music. One voice stood out above the rest. The Pastor hired him that week as the Cantor. He was David Taft Kekuewa who is still the Cantor for the Parish. Later that year he was able to hire Steven Meyer as the Organist and Music Director. He also still serves in that ministry.

As to the seven minute homilies, that is still a work in progress, as in every parish. For St. Vincent de Paul it still remains the goal each week. We are praised when we succeed.

The involvement of the laity has always been a work in progress. The goal is to have sufficient Lectors and Eucharistic Ministers and Ushers and Altar Servers for every Mass. Due to modern mobility, the list is a changing list. The parish has been blessed with outstanding people who have involved themselves in liturgical ministries and all other ministries and forms of community outreach. A group of Home-Visitors was formed to care for the sick and the housebound and bring Communion to them. In 1914 Archbishop Riordan had asked the parish to have a *"banner branch"* of the St. Vincent de Paul Society. In 1987 Charles Giampaoli and Dan Flanagan were the *"branch."* Then William Terheyden and Robert Baldocchi and Dave Des Marais joined them in attracting many more members to serve the needy and make the parish's St. Vincent de Paul Conference truly a *"banner branch."*

The first meeting of the Board of Presidents, similar to the Coordinating Committee talked of in previous years, was held on May 26, 1987. On an annual or special needs basis, the presidents or chairs of all parish groups were to meet with the Pastor 1) to review all the activities of the previous year and discuss any difficulties that occurred; 2) to hear from the Pastor a report on the parish spiritually and financially, as well as to question him on any aspect of parish life; and 3) to plan the calendar for the year to avoid any conflicts and to seek areas of collaboration rather than duplication.

After the Listening and Learning Session on Evangelization, the issue of education was immediately addressed. To stabilize the school financially, on February 19, 1987 an ad hoc committee on school finances and tuition was formed by the Pastor and the Principal, Sister Ann Conlon, PBVM. An open meeting of school parents was scheduled for February 26th. Discussion at the meeting centered on tuition and the fact that, even with a substantial subsidy from the parish, tuition would have to be raised significantly and eventually become the school's primary source of revenue.

In regard to care of the property, an ad hoc committee was formed of parishioners Roy Borgonovo, Bert Rodgers, Gene De Martini, and Mario Alioto. They were asked to study and advise the Pastor in regard to buildings and properties. Part of the study centered on the boilers. The Personnel Committee, in their December visitation in 1986, noted there was no heat in the rectory. On October 13, 1987 the rectory boiler was replaced as well as the boilers for the church and the school. A study also began on the problem of pigeons who made the parish property, especially the church, their home.

A civic event drew considerable attention to the parish area on May 24, 1987. It was the 50th birthday of the Golden Gate Bridge. For the second time in its history the bridge was closed to automobiles so people could walk across it as they had done on opening day.

A church event drew even greater attention on September 17th and 18th – the visit of Pope John Paul II to San Francisco. The helicopter bringing him from the airport flew over the parish and landed at Crissy Field. After a visit to the Golden Gate Bridge and Mission Dolores, the Pope had a meeting with the Religious and one with the Laity at St. Mary's Cathedral. Some of our parishioners were at the meeting for the laity. The main celebration, however, was a Mass at Candlestick Park. One of our parishioners, Bert Keane, coordinated this parish's participation. At 6:00 a.m. a procession of four buses and 33 cars took 310 parishioners to the festivities and the 10:45 a.m. Mass. The rest of the parish had to participate by television. And some, in doing so, saw a Mass at St. Vincent de Paul with Father Ring as the celebrant as well as the commentator. It was taped in July so one of the stations would have fill-in material for any lull in the Papal ceremonies.

November 8th saw the introduction of a *"Mass in the Contemporary Mode."* With piano, flute and guitar Barbara Bergson, Susan Wollan, Mark McCarthy, and Tracy Muller began a tradition at the Sunday 5:15 Mass for Young Adults.

Educationally the year saw the administration of the school for the first time in the hands of a layman. Mr. George Enes replaced Sister Ann as Principal. Religious were still on the faculty in the person of Sister Ange Cadigan BVM, and later Sister Noella Cavallero BVM. Along with the rest of the staff they helped for a smooth transition.

It was also the year for another first: girls as altar servers.

Also in the area of liturgy, an Organ Committee was established. Studies were made of organs locally and out of state. Requests for proposals were sent to eight organ builders throughout the nation.

As to the care of the property, long-awaited maintenance was done in the rectory and, for the sake of the church and the health of the parishioners, the pigeon issue was revisited. In June, the church was cleaned through high water pressure, and a substance called "Hot-foot" was applied to discourage pigeons from alighting on the church.

The major development of this time was the full involvement of the laity in decision and policy-making in the parish. A School Board and a School Finance Committee were introduced in the school. For the broader parish, a Parish Pastoral Council began to meet regularly with the Pastor to share in parish development. A Parish Finance Committee was formed to oversee all parish finances. These four committees became essential elements of the parish of St. Vincent de Paul.

In 1989 Father Ring found these committees very helpful, because he had added responsibilities. He was appointed as the Dean and a member of the Council of Priests and the College of Consultors to the Archbishop. There was much work to be done.

And then came October 17, 1989, 5:04 p.m. The earth shook and we shook – again. Parish properties suffered only minor damages, but the people of the parish suffered. Some died: one in the fire, others later because of the shock of the earthquake. No one's life went unchanged.

In 1906 the Pastor, Father Ryan, wrote nothing about the fire and earthquake. In 1957, Father O'Kane wrote only a few sentences. Mindful of this precedence, Father Ring wrote 29 pages! Entitled: *"Memories of the Earthquake of October 17, 1989,"* it has not been published. Less than a handful of people have read it; until the writing of this parish history, Father Ring had not re-read it since it was written. Rather than have it outweigh other events over the 100 years, it is now printed for the first time as an appendix to this history of St. Vincent de Paul.

One interesting footnote is not included in the history of the '89 earthquake: because they came so close to falling, the old plaster Stations of the Cross were removed and put in storage. They were replaced by the wood ones from the lower church, carved by Frederick Mussner of Livorno, Italy. Soon afterwards, Father Ring was visited by his classmate Bishop Tomas Camacho of Saipan. He was looking for Stations of the Cross for his Cathedral, and our plaster ones were just what he was looking for! If you are ever in the Northern Mariana Islands, visit the Cathedral of Our Lady of Mount Carmel in Chalon, Kanoa and you will see our Stations of the Cross.

As one reads *"Memories of the Earthquake"* one can see how easy it was for the parish and its people never to be the same. They had all suffered together. Now they were able to live together and work together and worship together with greater unity and devotion and enthusiasm.

The last decade of the Millennium and of St. Vincent de Paul's first hundred years is the story of a parish living and working and worshipping together in these ways. The story of the last ten years is told through the priorities of the parish: liturgy, education, involvement of the laity, and the care of the property entrusted to us.

In the documents of the Second Vatican Council we are told the Liturgy is *"the summit toward which the activity of the Church is directed and the fountain from which all her power flows."* In this decade, emphasis was put on offering warm and welcoming liturgies. Great time was spent in the recruitment and training of lectors, Eucharistic ministers, altar servers, musicians, and choir. The place of worship received high priority. The need for church improvements was already noted by Monsignor Clasby. The directives of the Second Vatican Council had already called for changes. Now the earthquake necessitated some changes and opened the door to doing even more to make the church more conducive to the Liturgy.

An open parish meeting was held in November 1989 to hear the desires and the dreams as well as some *"caveats"* and *"Thou shalt nots"* of the parishioners. With the information gathered, planning began with the Frank Portman Company as contractor and John D. Walsh as architect.

As the interior planning proceeded, Bob Buckter was brought in as a color consultant for the exterior of all the properties. In the summer of 1990 the church, rectory, school and gymnasium were painted by Giampolini and Co. at a cost of $198,800.

At a meeting on September 10, 1990 a scale model of the church interior was shown. It was also shown to the parishioners on Sunday. After some revisions, the work of renovation began on June 17, 1991. After three months of worshipping in the downstairs church, the parishioners gathered for Mass in the renewed church on the Feast of St. Vincent de Paul, September 27, 1991. Archbishop Quinn came to dedicate it and bless the new altar on November 3, 1991.

The Archbishop and parishioners found that the primary focus was on the altar and the ambo. This was achieved by their elevation and their being crafted in golden oak, in contrast to the darkened fir of the reredos and the ceilings. A new reredos with a *baldocchino* or canopy was added as a focusing wall;

vertically to draw attention down from the ceiling to the altar, and horizontally to draw attention from the other windows to the central one depicting the main mystery of our Faith, the Resurrection. Documents on the liturgy called for a unity and harmony of the furnishings with the architecture of the structure. A striking feature of the 1913 church was use of the corbel, the carved wooden brackets or braces that seem to support the ceiling all the way down the nave. This corbel design is used in the new reredos, the altar, the ambo, and the light fixtures as a unifying feature.

Liturgical documents on renovation also encourage a blending of the old and the new. The flower and plant stands are made from parts of the old white wood altar. Parts of the old wood altar rail form the prie-dieu before Mary and Joseph as well as the stands for the four old statues in the rear of the church. Even the six candlesticks were parts of the old altar. The statues of Mary and Joseph are new. They were hand-carved in Ortisei in the Bolzano area of the Italian Alps. The Reconciliation Chapels are also new and offer to the penitent the opportunity to confess face-to-face or behind the screen made of frosted glass.

While the church was being renovated, a new pipe organ was being built. A committee composed of Steven Semes, Steven Meyer and Father Ring consulted with many people and visited many organs. Visser-Rowland was awarded the contract on December 6, 1988. An Organ Fund was established; the goal of $200,000 was reached through many donations and one generous bequest by Barbara Holt. The organ was first used for the Christmas Liturgies of 1992. There are 23 stops of 30 ranks and 1,658 pipes. The pipes were made in Germany and Holland, the console and internal parts in Houston. Archbishop Quinn dedicated the organ on February 7, 1993 and played the inaugural piece, followed by a recital by Kenneth Z. Mansfield, assisted by Steven Meyer and his Golden Gate Boys Choir and Bellringers.

As part of St. Vincent de Paul's emphasis on music and liturgy, there were many concerts over the following years with organ and piano and pan-flute and guitar, as well as family liturgies and weekly Liturgies of the Word for children and monthly communal Anointings of the Sick.

During these years all the Liturgies in which parishioners shared were important. Four stand out historically; two were not held here. One was the Mass at Candlestick Park in 1987 with the Pope; the other was the Jubilee Mass 2000 with Archbishop Levada at Pac Bell Park in the pouring rain. Of the Masses in the parish church, the first was the Mass Archbishop Quinn offered with the parishioners on the Friday after the earthquake in 1989. The second was the standing-room only Funeral Mass for Father Lewis B. O'Neil, SJ on September 18, 2000. Father had served as Parochial Vicar here for 11 years before dying of cancer. Archbishop Levada presided and Father Ring preached the homily. Concelebrating with them were Bishop John Wester and the other Parochial Vicars, Father William Myers and Father Benjamin Nombrado, and two of Father O'Neil's close friends, Father Eugene Duggan and Father Edward Bohnert, and others as well.

To assist with Liturgies for children and to develop their prayer life and their religious education, a new position was added to the staff: a Pastoral Associate for Religious Formation. Over the years Sister Sharon Casey, OP, Sister Maura O'Donovan, CHF, Sister M. Antonio Heaphy, PBVM, and Sister Sheila Donegan, PBVM, have served in this position. For the children, this Associate bridges liturgy and education.

The question is still asked, "Are there nuns in the schools?" We can answer that we are grateful now to have a nun as Pastoral Associate, who assists the children and is also a resource person for all laity staffing St. Vincent de Paul School. The school, however, went from up to 12 Daughters of Charity as teachers, with one as Principal, to Sister Ann as Principal. Then Sister Ann moved and for the first time St. Vincent de Paul School did not have a nun as Principal.

On September 1, 1988 George Enes became the Principal and remained until June 1997. Sadly, a short Principalship followed. Claude C. Gibney began as Principal in August 1997. He was diagnosed with lymphoma and then leukemia in the weeks after Christmas. He died on April 6, 1998 and was buried from St. Vincent de Paul on Wednesday of Holy Week. Claude asked for Barbara Harvey, who had been teaching eighth grade since 1990, as interim principal. She was appointed Acting Principal upon his death She then applied for the position and was chosen from the candidates as the next Principal and was appointed in May 1998.

Much advancement was achieved through the tenure of these three Principals. The Kindergarten was brought from its isolated classroom into the primary building. A stronger distinction was made between the primary school and the junior high school. A computer lab was developed; the music program was enhanced. A Spanish teacher was hired and a program developed for every grade. A learning specialist and a drama program were added. What was the *"old Kindergarten room"* and then the Bottom Drawer Thrift Shop of the Auxiliary to de Paul Youth became the new Science Center.

During these years almost $150,000 was spent in removing asbestos from the cafeteria and then remodeling it with an acoustic ceiling, a new floor and fresh paint. $185,000 was spent on modernizing the junior high school building with new windows, lowered ceilings, and new lighting and flooring. New lockers were also installed.

All the work in the school was completed shortly before the celebration of the 75th Anniversary of St. Vincent de Paul School. On October 16, 1999 a Dinner Dance was held in the gymnasium for over 400 alumni. On Sunday, October 17th Archbishop William J. Levada was the main celebrant of the Jubilee Mass. One of the graduates of the school, Bishop Pierre Du Maine of San Jose, preached the homily. Concelebrating with the priests of the parish were other graduates of the school: Father Francis Frugoli, SJ, Father E. Hartwick Sullivan, CM, Father James Torrens, SJ, Father Robert Kevin White, and Father Edwin Harris, SJ. A reception and open house followed.

The parish's emphasis on education applied to adults as well as children. A major program offered each year was the Lenten Series. Some noted speakers and important topics included:

1987   Rev. Milton Walsh, Professor of Theology, St. Patrick's Seminary:
       Christ and the Church Today

1988   Rev. Randy Calvo, Judicial Vicar of Archdiocese:
       The Role of the Laity in the Modern World

1989   Rev. Robert McElroy, Professor at St. Patrick's Seminary:
       Modern Moral Issues

1990   Rev. Ronald Witherup, S.S., Professor of Scripture at St. Patrick's:
       The Bible

1991   Rev. Jack Bonsor, Professor of Theology at St. Patrick's:
       Foundations of our Faith

1992   Rev. Gerald Coleman, S.S., Rector of St. Patrick's:
       What the Church Teaches

1993   Archbishop Quinn and Bishops Sevilla and McGrath:
       The Bishops Speak

1994   Fr. Kenan Osborne, O.F.M., Professor and Author:
       Lay Ministry in the Church Today

1995   George Wesolek, Stephen Finn, Nat Wilburn, Rev. David Pettingill:
       The Pastoral Plan of the Archdiocese

1997   Rev. Michael Harriman, Sister Glenn Anne, O.P., Frank Hudson,
        George Wesolek, Rev. John Talesfore:
        The Call to Lead, Educate, Serve, and Worship

1998   Rev. John K. Ring, Rev. Lewis O'Neil, Rev. Joseph Bradley:
        The Sacraments

1999   Rev. John Talesfore, Rev David Pettingill, Ed and Peggy Gleason:
        Reconciliation and Peace

In addition to this Lenten Series, many parishioners shared in the School of Pastoral Leadership classes. During the time Father Edward Bohnert served as Parochial Vicar the parish also offered study groups on the *"Catechism of the Catholic Church,"* and at the same time Father Lewis B. O'Neil, SJ offered a weekly Bible Study. And they both were bridges from adults to children because they were both deeply involved in the school and all the activities of the school community.

From 1993 to 1995 Father Ring, in addition to his parish responsibilities, was one of the 13 members of the Archdiocesan Pastoral Planning Commission. Through parish consultations, visitations, studies, and surveys they offered a comprehensive pastoral plan for the Archdiocese. Father Ring was one of the principal drafters of *"A Journey of Hope Toward the Third Millennium – The Pastoral Plan of the Pilgrim Church of San Francisco."* It was promulgated on December 15, 1995.

One of the unhappy but necessary parts of the Pastoral Plan was the closing of some churches. St. Vincent de Paul had the responsibility of welcoming some people from St. Edward's and St. Brigid's. To assist those who found it difficult to get here, the parish offered free door-to-door van service to two of the Sunday Masses. Those who accepted the welcome fit easily into their new community of St. Vincent de Paul.

During the final decade of the Millennium and of St. Vincent de Paul's Centenary, it was not just the priests who were involved. The laity of the parish were very involved individually and through the various parish organizations.

During these years the de Paul Seniors, in their younger years known as the *Swinging Sixties*, were an important link for hundreds of people to the parish. To all of these were offered times for prayer and bingo, for pastries after Masses and luncheons on holidays, for trips to the theater and to Reno and beyond. Guided by good leaders and faithful workers over the years, this group has helped many to identify with St. Vincent de Paul.

The Auxiliary to de Paul Youth has been the fundraisers for the parish's gym program for youth of the area. Noel Balls at the Fairmont, fashion shows at the St. Francis Yacht Club, silent auctions with luncheons at Lehr's Greenhouse and then the Parish Hall were sources of other income. Through much hard work a thrift shop called the Bottom Drawer, located first in the basement of the convent and then the vacant convent and finally the old Kindergarten room, helped the sports program financially for many years.

The Parents' Guild, called the Seton Family Guild until recently, offers opportunities for parents of the parish school to gather together and share their ideas, as well as be educated in their Faith and parenting. Spring festivals, the *Under the Big Top* fashion show at the Hyatt Regency and the *Renaissance and Roses* fashion show at the Grand Hyatt, the *Toast to the New Year* cocktail party at the Presidio Officers Club and the *Toast to Teachers* wine tasting at the Golden Gate Yacht Club, all helped to involve the school community in St. Vincent de Paul.

Crab Cioppino dinners and Thanksgiving and Easter breakfasts were the identification marks of the Men's Club. This group involved people of all ages through annual parish picnics at Baywood Canyon Park in Fairfax and Morton's Warm Springs in Kenwood and the Windsor Water Slides. In this decade they also reintroduced a golf tournament at the Presidio Golf Club and Lincoln Park for men and women of the parish and their friends.

The Italian Catholic Federation has been important in gathering together those of Italian ancestry as well as others. On November 4, 1995 they celebrated at the Italian Athletic Club the 60th anniversary of their involvement at St. Vincent de Paul. It offered the opportunity to thank them for using proceeds of their dinners and bake sales to offer tuition assistance to graduates of our school each year.

The parish St. Vincent de Paul Conference helps parishioners to imitate our patron saint. They help the needy of our city through offering fresh fruit and sandwiches to homeless centers and shelters for battered women. Their presence is known at the Vincentian Desk, the Ozanam Center, the Arlington Hotel, and Rosalie House. St. Vincent de Paul Parish has a second collection every month for the poor. The Conference allots the money raised to the poor.

The Young Adult Group, once known as the Greensteiners, was revitalized on April 29, 1991 by Delly Tamer and others. Emphasis was placed on the spiritual, the social, and service to the community. Lectures and interactive presentations, Masses and retreats at Marconi Center and Vallombrosa have been part of the spiritual program. Dinners and the ballet, ski weekends and white water rafting drew the group together socially. Service to the community has included tutoring children in the Tenderloin, visiting the elderly each week at the Heritage, working with the St. Vincent de Paul Conference on the fresh fruit program every Saturday and the Share-Bag program at Thanksgiving, and taking children of the Tenderloin to Giants' games and the zoo, as well as playing Santa Claus for them with presents from the parish's Giving Tree. A highlight of their Monday night meetings was when Archbishop Quinn spoke to and listened to 150 of them at their May 23, 1994 meeting about their role in the church. Their involvement was acknowledged and appreciated.

There have been other ways and other groups through which people have been involved with St. Vincent de Paul over the past decade. At the beginning of the decade as well as at the end, RENEW has been an important source of involvement and renewal. There is the continuing program of the de Paul Youth Club, which involves not only children of the school but also neighborhood children in activities in our gymnasium. There was an attempt at Youth Ministry for teenagers, but their involvement in their high schools made participation too difficult. There was also a "35 to 40-Something" group that was successful for a time. A Young Married Group was popular and then faltered; it is now beginning again.

The desire to involve people of the parish through the many individual organizations has been blessed by the organizations working collaboratively with one another. This unity has been manifested in a special way each year since 1997 in the Parish Mardi Gras, a dinner-dance for the whole parish, prepared and presented by all the parish organizations together. The hundreds attending each year can attest that the people of St. Vincent de Paul enjoy being involved with one another.

Another community builder is a dinner the parish hosts each January to honor all those involved in the liturgical ministries of the parish. Among the 200 people receiving invitations to this event are Eucharistic Ministers, lectors, choir members, instrumentalists, ushers, marriage preparation leaders, baptismal catechists, home visitors for the sick, and directors of liturgies for children. Welcoming them are the Parish Pastoral Council, Finance Committee, presidents of parish organizations and parish staff.

Over the years many people have been involved through organizations and also as individuals. Primary among these are members of the staff who serve the people of the parish, including parish secretaries Margaret Carroll and Mae Watters; in more recent years, Christine Martino Hein, who got the non-typing

Pastor through his years with the Pastoral Planning Commission; and current secretary Kathleen Mulhern, who through her personal and computer skills has helped the Pastor and the Parish in these difficult recent years and now in preparation for the Centennial. And blessed is this parish for our receptionist, Juanita Arfsten, who has worked with every Pastor except Father Ryan. She was active in Father Long's days and drove him during his sick years. She was in the Altar Society and began to work part-time in the parish office in Father O'Kane's years. Juanita started full-time as receptionist with Monsignor Clasby and continues in this position with Father Ring. Blessed is St. Vincent de Paul with such dedicated and involved people.

Care of the properties entrusted to us is the fourth parish priority. During the past decade, this has been trying and expensive.

As we have seen, the church, rectory, school, and gymnasium were painted in the summer of 1990. At that time, an attempt was also made to re-landscape the property. Because of the neighbors' protests about removal of four eucalyptus trees whose roots were making the sidewalks hazardous, the City refused to grant a permit for two years. On the day it was granted at the end of July 1992, one of our parishioners, Joseph Figone, had the four trees down before sunset. The following week he planted five ficus and some magnolias to replace them. The whole sidewalk was then replaced and the central parking lot repaved before school opened at the end of August.

Over the years neighborhood problems also developed over the closure of Green Street for the school children to play at recess and lunch hour. It was a permission granted by the Board of Supervisors on September 26, 1927 and approved by Mayor James Rolph, Jr. on October 7, 1927. It was questioned without success in 1970. In 1997, with much publicity, the City of San Francisco was sued for closing a public street for parochial school students and allegedly allowing double parking for church services. The suit failed.

It was not the first time that difficulties in parking at St. Vincent de Paul came to public attention. All the way back in Father Ryan's time, an item appeared on July 2, 1941 in one of San Francisco's daily papers:

> *The automobile crowd at St. Vincent de Paul Church at Green and Steiner is so great Sunday mornings that attendants double-park their cars all along the block to the distress of a big policeman at that point. So last Sunday morning he growled to no one in particular, "What we need, I can see, is drive-in churches!*

In 1989 and 1990 asbestos was removed from the cafeteria and remodeling done.

In 1991 the church interior was remodeled (as related earlier) at a cost of $385,000, most of which was raised by a Renovation Fund.

In 1992 there was the landscaping and paving. (The Men's Club helped with the cost of the paving.)

In 1993, the Visser Rowland pipe organ was installed.

In 1994, the parish finally had to face the issue of the convent property. The Parish Pastoral Council and Finance Committee spent many hours in meeting and in consulting with parishioners. The neighbors and the City were also consulted at considerable length. The parish's desire was to demolish the convent and develop the property as a playground for the school and as a parking lot for the parish.

The demolition and development permits were granted in Spring 1994 and the convent was taken down on September 6, 1994. Frank Portman Co. was the contractor for that and for the grading and the improvement to the property. The cost was $180,000 for the entire playground/parking lot project. It was ready for use on December 18, 1994; unfortunately, the concerns and demands of neighbors were not resolved until November of 1995. Only then was the project completed.

Simultaneous with that project was development of the lower church. The area had started off as the church, and it became the parish hall in 1913. In 1953, it was needed as a downstairs chapel to accommodate the crowds. It was used only occasionally as such in the 1970s and 1980s. During the church remodeling in 1991, it served well as a chapel for three months. Now the people needed more meeting space. With Kevin Dill as architect and Frank Portman Co. as contractor, planning began in 1994.

1995 saw the development of one spacious parish hall that could, by sliding partitions, become three meeting rooms: the Chapel Room, which retained the altar and crucifix; the Pastors' Room, with historical pictures of the former Pastors and the church and school; and the Donors' Room, with pictures of those who donated over $50,000 to the parish. The renovation entailed new lighting, heating, flooring, and sound. The addition of toilets and a sprinkler system and handicapped accessibility was costly The whole project cost $385,000. Fortunately Charles Giampaoli, in addition to leaving considerable money to the School Endowment, funded the major part of this expense. The Parish Hall of St. Vincent de Paul had its Gala Opening on October 13, 1995.

1997 saw remodeling of the Junior High School, and foundation work on the Primary School. Underground springs had caused erosion over the years.

Aware of our responsibility in caring for the properties entrusted to us, the parish began to prepare for its Centenary in 1997. It established a Restoration Fund to insure the church was fit for the parish's birthday in 2001. One project triggered a second project, and the two projects occasioned a third project.

A new roof was needed. Roofing contractors and structural engineers were called in. The Parish Advisory Boards decided on a slate roof and new copper battans. The contract was won by Western Roofing; their work, including removal of the old asbestos shingle roof, some reconstruction work, the slate shingle roof with copper battans, and the scaffolding cost $470,617. Painting the exterior, by Monticelli Painting, was $84,754. Pigeon-proofing the church with netting and wires cost $24,840. That was only the beginning.

When the parish applied to the City for permits for the roof, we were informed we could not proceed without making the church handicapped accessible. Although the timing was not good, it actually was a need we wanted to address. We also needed to replace the entrance stairs that were cracked through settling. To do the roof, we had to do the ramp, and we did not want to do the ramp without the stairs and the terrazzo sidewalk in front of the church. The cost: $265,785!

It was costly because so much foundation work had to be addressed. This unfortunately (future generations will say fortunately) triggered more studies. We were informed the retrofitting done after the 1957 earthquake did not satisfy current standards required by the City of San Francisco. Seismic work was necessary. There had to be additional foundation work and veneer anchoring and steel beams. Cahill Construction, together with Degenkolb Engineers, completed this work in 1999 for $392,127.

The Restoration Fund saved us – it received 632 donations from parishioners. Added to it was a $253,000 bequest from Marcella de Escudero. The balance came from savings and the second collections each month for development.

The final projects of the first hundred years included, in 2000 and 2001, painting the school exterior, new windows and painting the rectory exterior, and painting the gym's exterior and interior, as well as a new roof. Painting the church interior and refinishing the floor and pews will be the final preparation for celebration of the first hundred years of the parish of St. Vincent de Paul.

The final decade of people worshipping together, providing for education and formation, involving themselves in work and ministries, and caring for the property entrusted to them, makes them a people worthy of a celebration on earth and in eternity.

The 100th anniversary celebration will be a Gala Birthday Party for all parishioners and benefactors of St. Vincent de Paul on the afternoon of October 21, 2001. It is being coordinated by Mrs. Ruth DeLutis, Mrs. Maryanne Harrison, and Mrs. Mimi Ysturiz-Dougherty.

There will be a Jubilee Mass of Thanksgiving prior to the party. Presiding will be The Most Reverend William J. Levada, the Archbishop of San Francisco. Concelebrating with him will be Father John K. Ring and the other priests and former priests of the parish.

It will be a Mass of Thanksgiving for 100 years of the generous graces of God and of the countless blessings of the thousands of people who have been part of St. Vincent de Paul over the years. We will give thanks for the 7,671 Baptisms and 4,302 marriages and the 100,000 Masses that were celebrated at St. Vincent de Paul's during this first 100 years.

Proudly, as this history shows, the Parish of St. Vincent de Paul has fulfilled the challenging words of the American Bishops:

> *The Parish is where the Church lives.*
> *Parishes are communities of faith, of action, and of hope.*
> *They are where the Gospel is proclaimed and celebrated*
> *where believers are formed and sent to renew the earth.*
> *Parishes are the home of the Christian community.*
> *They are the heart of our church.*
> *Parishes are the place where God's people*
> *meet Jesus in Word and in Sacrament*
> *and come in touch with the source of the Church's life.*

Humbly the Parish of St. Vincent de Paul entrusts the people of the first hundred years and the priests and parishioners of the next hundred years into the hands of our Patron St. Vincent de Paul, as we pray:

St. Vincent de Paul,

as people of a parish named in your honor,

we recognize you as our patron and we ask for your help.

We ask you to intercede for us with our loving and compassionate Father.

We ask to be strengthened in the graces of our Baptism,

in the challenges of our Confirmation,

in our faithfulness to the Eucharist.

We ask for a strengthening of our faith in God,

in our hope for our world,

in our love for one another.

Through your intercession, we seek God's blessings

upon us and upon our families,

upon our Parish of St. Vincent de Paul and upon the Church of San Francisco

as we prepare for another hundred years of service to God and one another,

Seek for us the graces we need

to be true to the Gospel, true to the Church, true to our Faith.

Help us to draw others to Christ, to care for all of God's children,

and to be sensitive to the needs of the poor in our midst and

throughout the world.

Intercede for us in our great need for vocations to service

as priests and sisters and brothers and committed members of the laity.

Through your pleas for us at the throne of God,

may our Parish of St. Vincent de Paul and all of its people,

in this Centennial Year and the years to come,

be signs of the holiness and joy of God

forever and ever.

We ask this as always through Christ our Lord.

Amen.

Father John K. Ring

Installation of Father Ring 1987

Archbishop Quinn at the Installation of Father Ring

Archbishop Quinn at Installation

Papal Mass at Candlestick Park 1987

Renovation of Church

Remodeled Church 1991

Remodeled Church 1991

Dedication of remodeled Church 1991

Christ the King Window

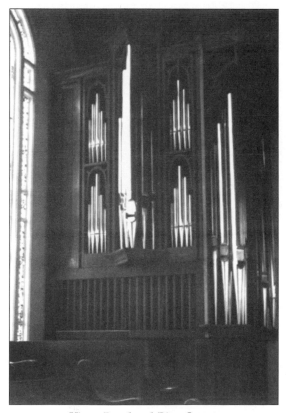

Visser-Rowland Pipe Organ

Organ dedicated 1993

Demolition of Convent 1994

Dedication of new Parish Hall 1995

New Parish Hall

Hall used as Chapel, Summer 1999

First Communion Class 1995

Painting of Church 1998

Seismic work 1999

Father Ring, Archbishop Levada, Bishop DuMaine
75th Anniversary of School

75th Anniversary of School

Mardi Gras Celebration

Mardi Gras Celebration

Mardi Gras Celebration

Mardi Gras Celebration

Chefs of St. Vincent de Paul 1990s

First Communion 1997

Graduates of 1997

RCIA Group 1998

Juanita Arfsten
Kathleen Mulhern

Church of St. Vincent de Paul 2001

St. Vincent de Paul 2001

Priests who have served the Church of St. Vincent de Paul 1901–2001

The Reverend:

Martin P. Ryan	1901–1941
Lawrence Murphy	1902–1907
John Harrington	1905
Michael Crotty	1907–1909
Egisto Tozzi	1909–1913
John Powers	1909–1915
Patrick Heslin	1911–1915
James Cantwell	1911
Peter Flynn	1913–1917
Peter Bennett	1914–1915
A Kevany	1915–1917
James Long	1917–1923, 1930–1951
James Donohoe	1917–1920
Thomas F. Butler	1920
Patrick Kennedy	1920–1921
Thomas Brady	1922
Edward McCarthy	1922
B Dempsey	1922–1923
Thomas Cummins	1923–1925
Frances Dougherty	1923–1925
James McHugh	1925
William Walsh	1925–1927
John Scanlon	1925–1926
Martin Egan	1926–1930
Richard O'Connell	1927–1930
Albert Duffy	1929
Thomas I. Bresnahan	1929–1936
Peter Doherty	1930
Patrick Morris	1930–1934
William Hennessy	1934–1935
Nicholaus P. Connolly	1934
James McElligott	1935–1943

Patrick Thompson	1936
James J. O'Donnell	1936–1943
John D. Curran	1937
Raymond W. Kenny	1938–1943
Thomas N. O'Kane	1941–1943, 1951–1964
Clyde Tillman	1943–1951
John P. Connolly	1943–1957
Daniel P. Shea	1943–1945
Robert Hayburn	1945–1950
Joseph B. Schwab	1949–1953
Eugene F. Duggan	1951–1954
William R. Lowery	1953–1958
John C. Murphy	1954–1961
Francis K. Murray	1958–1964
James C. Concannon	1959—1961
John J. Cox	1961–1962
Frank K. Piro	1962–1966
Edward H. Andre	1964–1968
William J. Clasby	1965–1986
Robert S. Gorman	1966–1967
Michael W. Murray	1967–1969
Liam Tuohy	1968–1969
Austin Keegan	1969–1972
John J. Scanlon	1969–1971
Louis Robello	1969–1971
Terrence Sullivan	1971–1976
A. M. Muldoon	1972–1978
Lawrence J. Finegan	1974–1977
Anthony O'Brien	1977–1982
Michele Raimondi	1978–1988
Charles J. Sullivan	1981–1984
Harry G. Schlitt	1982–1983
Clifford A. Martin	1984-1987
John K. Ring	1987–Present
Alex L. Legaspi	1987–1991
Joseph Richard	1987–1989
Lewis B. O'Neil	1989–2000
Edward Bohnert	1993–1998
Joseph Bradley	1998
Richard Mandoli	1998–1999
William Myers	2000–2001
Benjamin A. Nombrado	2000–Present

Principals who have served the School of St. Vincent de Paul 1924-2001

Sister Barbara Murphy, DC	1924–1928
Sister Mary Michael Ryan, DC	1928–1933
Sister Anne Casey, DC	1933–1938
Sister Winifred Driscoll, DC	1938–1943
Sister Marguerite Harrington, DC	1943–1949
Sister Emily O'Flaherty, DC	1949–1954
Sister Blanche Tucker, DC	1954–1958
Sister Genevieve Colman, DC	1958–1962
Sister Mary Genevieve Moonier, DC	1962–1968
Sister Emily O'Flaherty, DC	1968–1969
Sister Muriel Mountain, DC	1969–1975
Sister Germaine Sarrazin, DC	1975–1977
Sister Stella Joseph Burns, DC	1977–1983
Sister Frances Meyer, DC	1983–1986
Sister Ann Conlan, PBVM	1986–1988
Mr. George Enes	1988–1997
Mr. Claude C. Gibney	1997–1998
Mrs. Barbara J. Harvey	1998–Present

The Story of the
Stained Glass Windows
of
St. Vincent De Paul Church

St. Vincent de Paul Church
San Francisco, California

"Christ the King" Window

Why the Stained Glass Window?

Prominent among places of interest for travelers in Europe are the great cathedrals. Even otherwise insignificant towns are known the world over because of a glorious sermon in wood or stone. These magnificent temples of God are as so many silent witnesses to the great faith of the people who built them. Churches were built in the form of a cross to remind men of the principal event in man's redemption. Graceful towers were lifted into the sky to direct men's minds above the little things of earth to God. And with the invention of the stained glass window, sunlight was utilized to illustrate the principal teachings, events and persons in the Divine Story.

Your Parish church, dedicated to the honor and glory of God and bearing the name of a great priest, St. Vincent de Paul, was meant from the beginning to be in harmony with this great tradition in the Church. Consequently, in the original design, provision was made for stained glass windows. Only now is it possible to begin this part of the original plan. The first of the stained glass windows has just been installed.

This first stained glass window in the church honors Christ the King. Certainly this is a most fitting theme. Christ is the Lord of the world. To Him the world owes complete allegiance. He is the Divine Lawgiver. All Men are bound to love and obey Him. He is "the Blessed and Almighty, the King of kings and Lord of lords."

Central Panel — "Christ the King"

In the central panel of the window there is the magnificent figure of Christ in all His Kingly glory. On His head He wears a golden regal crown. He is robed in royal garments. His hands are raised to bless. Beneath His feet is the earth, His possession. Christ, the King! This is the theme of the whole window, to which all else that is represented refers. Beneath the figure of Christ the King there is a medallion, which pictures our Lord's Ascension into Heaven. The figures of the Apostles, in their many colored vestments, gaze up at their Lord, returning to His Heavenly Father and to the glory that was His own before the world began.

East Panel — Old Testament

To the East of the central panel is a lancet which, in three scenes, portrays Old Testament prophecy or prefigurement of the Kingship of Christ. In the lowest medallion there is represented the scene wherein the Patriarch Abraham stands before Melchisedech, who has always been regarded as a type of Christ, not merely because of his priesthood, but also because of his titles, "King of Justice" and "King of Peace."

In the center medallion we find a scene from the First Book of Kings, the Prophet Samuel anointing young David. *"Then Samuel took the horn of oil, and anointed him in the midst of his brethren."* This anointing was done at the bidding of God Himself, and it represents the choice of David as King of the Jews in place of Saul, whom God has rejected. David, the great God-fearing ruler, typifies Christ, "the anointed One," the King of Kings.

In the top medallion is an illustration of the Psalm by David which refers directly to the future Messianic King: *"The Lord said to my Lord: Sit thou at my right hand until I make thy enemies thy footstool."* God the Father is seated on a throne, with Christ standing at His side, scepter in hand. Beneath the feet of Christ is the figure of a devil, representing all that is inimical to God. The idea of the Kingship of Christ is very clearly demonstrated.

West Panel — New Testament

The lancet to the West of the central panel portrays three scenes from the New Testament, which have a very real connection with the central theme of the whole window. The medallion at the bottom is a representation of the incident in Our Lord's life wherein His power over all things is strikingly manifested. A raging storm on Lake Genesareth has brought great fear to the Apostles, who are crossing by boat with Christ from one side to the other. By a simple command Christ stills the waters. *"Even the wind and sea obey Him."*

The center medallion reveals the joyful, triumphant entry of Christ into Jerusalem. The people strew their garments along His way, and wave olive branches in their hands. They welcome Him as their King. It is in describing this scene that the Evangelist refers to the Old Testament prophecy, *"Behold, thy king comes, sitting on an ass's colt."*

The topmost scene in this side lancet shows Christ standing before Pilate on the first Good Friday. The Roman official asks of him: *"Thou art then a king?"* Jesus answered, *"Thou sayest it: I am a king."*

The Rose Window

Surmounting all the rest is the Rose Window. On its outer circle are pictured adoring angels, and the Christian symbol of peace, the dove. In the very center there is a figure representing God the Father. Above this there is the figure of a dove in representation of the Holy Spirit. In this manner, there is introduced the great doctrine of our Faith, the Holy Trinity.

∼

This, in brief, is the window in honor of Christ the King. Beautiful in its figures, its details and its colors it is, above all else, replete with the teachings of God's Church. It is a fitting adornment. It will be a reminder to those to come, of the Faith of the builders of the church and of their love for the house of the Lord. *"I have loved, O Lord, the beauty of thy house; and the place where thy glory dwelleth."*

The Papacy Window

How could one speak of the teaching of the Divine Master without making mention of the Papacy, which He gave to be the unerring guide of the faithful, the visible representation of Himself? Or as St. Ambrose so succinctly put it, *"Where Peter is there is the Church."*

In the Papacy Window, which is third on the Epistle side of the nave of the church, there is portrayed the unforgettable and ever-challenging scene wherein Christ promised Peter that He would make him the rock upon which His Church would be built; where He promised that He would give him infallible power to bind and loose on earth; where He set aside fears on human frailty with the assurance that the assaults of the devil would fall harmlessly on the strong structure that is His Church. It is most interesting to notice certain details present in the beautiful window: the rock, symbol of the Church; the keys, symbol of infallibility; the wheat field, symbol of the souls of the faithful; and in the border the tiara, unique crown of the successors of Peter.

Very appropriate is the subject choice for the medallion in this window. We see Noah standing beside the finished Ark, just before the deluge overflowed the earth, which had become so displeasing to God by sin. And the Lord said to him: *"go in thou and all thy house into the ark."* The Church founded by Christ is the Ark of Salvation for all men, and Christ speaks to all, even as God spoke to Moses: *"go in thou and all thy house into the ark."*

The window depicting the Papacy is in pious memory of Lorraine McDonnell; the window of the Holy Spirit is in holy memory of Vincent John Gartland.

The Holy Spirit Window

Our God is a Triune God. Here is but one God, yet in that one God there are three distinct Divine Persons, each possessing the same Divine Nature. It was Christ, the Second Person in this Blessed Trinity, who promised to send the Holy Spirit, the Third Divine Person, upon His Church, *"who will teach you all things,"* who is our Strength, our Vivifier, our Enlightener.

The stained glass window, the third on the Gospel side of the nave of the church, illustrates the first Pentecost, when the Holy Spirit descended, in the form of tongues of fire, upon the Blessed Mother and the Apostles in the upper room in Jerusalem. This was the day when timid men became fearless apostles, whom not even earthy men's greatest fear, death, could persuade to give up the planting of the Faith, and the harvesting of souls – for God.

In the medallion is Moses on Mt. Sinai, receiving the tablets, the Ten Commandments. Here is the Old Law, the Covenant of Promise. But the New Covenant is from Christ, The Fulfillment of the Promise, sealed with the coming of the Holy Spirit.

The Doubting-Thomas Window

Well might atheists, professors or otherwise, sit and ponder this window (the last window on the Epistle Side of the nave). Men, with men's minds, challenge God-told truths because they cannot see, understand fully what is told them. Thomas doubted, because his mind rejected what it could not comprehend. So Christ visited Thomas, to prove to him, and to all other doubters, that more than seeing is believing. *"Bring here thy finger...; bring here thy hand...; and be not unbelieving, but believing." "Thomas answered... 'My Lord and my God!' Jesus said to him, 'because thou has seen me, thou hast believed. Blessed are they who have not seen, and yet have believed.'"*

This particular window is most apropos to one of the principal aims of the windows of the church: to show forth the Divinity of Christ.

The medallion below shows the great Moses standing, in awe, barefoot out of reverence, before the burning bush in which God appeared to him. The Lord called to Moses; *"'Come not nigh hither, put off the shoes from thy feet: for the place whereon thou standest is holy ground...I am the God of thy father, the God of Abraham, the God of Isaac, and the God of Jacob.' Moses hid his face; for he durst not look at God."* This incident reminds one vividly of the awe one should feel in the presence of Jesus, the Son of God.

141

The Transfiguration Window

"Jesus took Peter, James and his brother, John, and led them up a high mountain by themselves, and was transfigured before them. And his face shone as the sun, and his garments became white as snow. And behold, there appeared to Him Moses and Elias talking together with Him...And behold, a voice out of the cloud said, 'This is my beloved Son, in whom I am well pleased; hear him.' And on hearing it the disciples fell on their face and were exceedingly afraid." It is this undeniable evidence of the Divinity of Christ that is pictured in the last window on the Epistle Side of the nave.

The medallion below shows an angel speaking to Daniel: *"O Daniel, I am now come forth to teach thee...Therefore do thou mark the work and understand the vision. Seventy weeks are shortened upon thy people, and upon the holy city, that transgression may be finished...and everlasting justice may be brought; and vision and prophecy may be fulfilled; and the saint of saints may be anointed."* Here is a foretelling of the coming of Christ, who is above all saints, the fulfillment of all prophecies, God Eternal.

The Cana Miracle Window

"These very works that I do bear witness to me." "Dost thou not believe that I am in the Father and the Father in me? Believe because of the works themselves." Men believe another when they are convinced that he is an honest man. Jesus did not disdain to give men many evidences of the fact that He is Truth Itself. His miracles are His way of irrefutably showing men that He is the Eternal Son of God. In the window, which faces the Blessed Mother altar, the scene is the miracle at the marriage feast in Cana. The main reason for the choice of this subject is to present a miracle of Christ, to show forth the more, His Divinity. Yet this particular scene is a happy choice for still another reason: it shows the high esteem in which our Lord held marriage, His love for the little people of this world, and even His approval of innocent enjoyment. The symbol on the shield in the border of the window refers to marriage: the "chi-rho" (XP) symbolizes Christian Marriage: Christ, husband, wife.

The medallion for this window shows Moses, after he had struck the rock with a rod, at the bidding of God. Water miraculously pours forth. The Jewish people, in their desert journey from Egypt to the Promised Land, were parched with thirst, and were complaining. Moses begged God's help. This particular scene shows very well that it is God alone who works miracles. Saints work them in the name and by the power of God. Christ works them in His own name, for He is God.

The Cure of the Paralytic Window

The window facing the St. Joseph altar depicts a second miracle performed by our Blessed Lord – another evidence of His Divinity. The paralytic is shown lifting himself, cured, from his bed of pain, at the wondrous word of Christ. Three figures stand a little apart. It is interesting to note the different reaction of each. Some men are humble and willingly accept the truth. Others are stubborn, even in the face of the obvious.

There is a secondary purpose in the choice of this particular scene from the life of Christ: The Divine Master had first forgiven the invalid his sins, and given His infinitely more precious blessing. The Scribes then accused him of blasphemy: *"Who can forgive sins, but God only?"* Christ thereupon worked the miracle of the cure, to show these men that He forgave sins precisely because He was God. In all of this we see, so plainly, the inestimable value of Our Lord's later gift to his children: Confession.

The medallion for this window shows the prophet Eliseus in the act of raising from the dead the son of a woman of the Sunamites. The grief-stricken woman and Giezi, the boy servant of the prophet, are also to be seen in the picture. Here again there is an evidence of the power of God in the world. In the prophet of the Old Testament God works through one of His creatures. Christ is God Himself working His own works.

The Story of the "Incarnation" Window

Whether it be in churches and cathedrals grown old in the service of God or in those newly dedicated to Him, it is the tradition of the Church to lay particular stress, in adorning the house of God, on certain major events in the life of our Lord. In so doing the Church knows that her children will have an effective reminder to understand and appreciate what they ought to know and love. Thus in stained glass, on canvas, in marble and wood, the faithful are told and retold all through their days of the Incarnation, the Passion, the Resurrection, the Ascension. These are the principal happenings in the life of the Saviour, serving to fix attention on the work of man's salvation, the love of God for men. It is easy to understand, therefore, why the third of the great windows in St. Vincent de Paul church commemorates the Incarnation, the humble beginning of the wondrous act of God's love for His creatures.

The Center Panel — The Incarnation

The faithful, young and old alike, have always found happiness in the contemplation of Bethlehem, the cave, Joseph, Mary and the Eternal Son of God, a tiny Baby wrapped in swaddling clothes. This is the main theme of the present window: the birth of the Saviour. Mary, the Mother, kneels in adoration. Joseph stands in reverent watch. God lies in a manger. Overhead the star points its myriad fingers to the spot where Divinity embraces Humanity. In His heaven sits the Father of the Divine Son, surrounded by heaven's ever adoring angels. The Dove, the Holy Spirit Who made Mary the Mother of God while keeping her a virgin, hovers over earth's Blessing. *"This day is born to you a Saviour who is Christ the Lord."*

In the medallion below is the scene of the Annunciation. The beautiful figure of the sinless virgin, kneeling in humble prayer, is visited by God's messenger, the Archangel Gabriel. *"My soul doth magnify the Lord...because He hath regarded the humility of His handmaid. For behold from henceforth all generations shall call me blessed."* Unknown to men, yet well loved by God, Mary is chosen to be the Mother of the Second Person of the Blessed Trinity. *"The Holy who shall be born of thee shall be called the Son of God."*

Left Panel — Old Testament

All through the pages of the Old Testament run the promise and the hope of the Saviour. In the present window three of the outstanding prophecies of the Redeemer are pictured. In the lowest medallion there is the scene in the Garden of Eden: God the Father speaks to the cringing Serpent, the Devil. He promises the Redeemer of mankind and pronounces the inescapable condemnation of the Powers of Hell. Adam and Eve, seen in the background, conscious of their guilt, had sinned and the world must suffer. Christ and Mary will come and sin shall know its Conqueror. *"I will put enmities between thee and the woman, and thy seed and her seed."*

In the center of the panel is represented the Promise of God to Abraham. The Patriarch stands before his tent. God has appeared to him in a cloud and assures him that the Redeemer shall come from his race: *"In thee shall all the kindred of the earth be blessed."*

The third of the Old Testament scenes presents the wonderful Promise of the Virgin Birth of the Saviour. Achaz, the Jewish king, has been threatened with disaster by his enemies. God sends His Prophet, Isaias, to remind him to place his trust in God. The Prophet bids Achaz to ask of God a sign of assurance. The foolish king, preferring to trust to the help of some royal friends, answers that he will not tempt God. Whereupon Isaias rebukes the king, and tells him that

144

God will give a sign nevertheless. *"Behold a virgin shall conceive, and bear a son, and his name shall be called Emmanuel."*

Right Panel — New Testament

There are depicted, in the right panel, three very familiar scenes from the New Testament. In the lowest medallion there is the Adoration of the Magi, long before foretold by the Psalmist: *"The kings of Tharsis and the islands shall offer presents: The kings of the Arabians and of Saba shall bring gifts."* Here is the first act of homage from the Gentiles: *"They found the child and His mother, and falling down they adored Him."*

In the center medallion there is recalled the presentation of the Child Jesus in the Temple. Simeon reverently holds the Infant in his arms. Mary stands watching, and Joseph, holding in his hands the offering of the poor, two doves in a little cage. The aged Simeon says his "nunc dimittis": *"My eyes have seen thy salvation."*

In the final medallion there is the story of the Flight into Egypt. Warned by heaven to flee from the persecution of the tyrant Herod, Joseph is seen leading the little beast of burden, bearing its precious burden, Mary, with the Divine Infant wrapped in her arms. The waters of the Nile and the pyramids give evidence that the Holy Family has reached the land of its exile.

The Rose Window

As a fitting crown for this homage in glass to the Incarnation is the beautiful Rose Window. In its center there is the figure of the Incarnate Son of God. Adoring angels offer their joyous hymn of praise. Off to one corner is enshrined the sign of Bethlehem, the Star. In the other corner is placed a burning candle, symbol of Christ, the Light of the World.

The title given to this, the last of the three great windows in the church, is most fitting. Briefly it reminds us that men shall know peace only as long as they keep God in their life: *"Peace on earth to men of good will."*

The Rose Window of the Incarnation Window is the generous gift of the Butte Family.

The Story of the
Mother of Divine Grace Window
and of the St. Vincent de Paul Window

The theme of the two new stained glass windows is in very real harmony with Church tradition. The window above the altar of the Blessed Virgin honors Mary, the Mother of Divine Grace. The window above the St. Joseph altar is in honor of St. Vincent de Paul, the patron saint of the parish.

Devotion to the Mother of God is, and always has been, prominent in the life of the Church, and in the lives of individual Catholics. This love for Mary has always been told in every conceivable and fitting manner, for such a love as this must find frequent and worthy expression. It would be an offense to the faithful of this Church were there to be no expression of this love through the beautiful medium of stained glass.

It is likewise fitting that there should be a window in honor of St. Vincent de Paul. Holy Mother Church asks of her children that they pay special homage to the patron saint of their parish church. Devout Catholics instinctively feel a particular devotion to the saint whose name their parish bears. It would be as a sin of omission to fail to honor St. Vincent de Paul with the constant and beautiful voice of the stained glass of the Church.

The "Mother of Divine Grace" Window

Artists of every age have spent lavishly of their talents to picture, on canvas, in fresco, in marble, stone and glass, the Mother of God. No other human person has ever captured their imagination as she has. Nor is this to be wondered at, for which of God's creatures can compare with her, the paragon of virtue, *"our tainted nature's solitary boast"*. Here is one further effort to pay homage to the spotless Virgin, under the title of "Mother of Divine Grace." Graceful, beautiful, immaculate, she stands with arms extended. For her crown are the seven stars of which St. John speaks in the Apocalypse. She looks with loving, watchful eyes upon her children; from her hands stream countless rays of light, indicative of the endless pouring out upon her own of the Graces won by her Divine Son. The Mediatrix of all Grace! The stainless channel of the Graces so necessary for the souls of men! From her virginal flesh the Redeemer came into the world of men. From her pure hands issue forth the Redeemer's priceless gifts of Grace.

Beneath the figure of Mary is a medallion picturing the dream of Jacob. In his sleep Jacob was shown a ladder reaching from heaven to earth, and angels ascending and descending thereon. This ladder has been accepted, from the time of the early Fathers of the Church, as a figure of Mary, through whom our prayers ascend to God in heaven, and through whom God's Graces come down to give life and nourishment to the souls of men. It is interesting to note in the border design of the window the coat of arms of Pope Pius V. In miniature in the center of the border on either side it reminds us of a Pope whose great devotion to the Mother of God was evidenced by the introduction of a feast in her honor and by earnest effort to spread devotion to her Rosary.

The "St. Vincent de Paul" Window

St. Vincent de Paul was born of poor parents, in 1576, in Southeastern France. His was rather a quiet childhood; then years of study, when often he had to tutor to pay his expenses; sturdy piety, eventuating in the call to the Priesthood; further hardships, because of financial difficulties; finally, the Priesthood, on September 13, 1600. Very shortly after his ordination Vincent, while traveling by sea from Marseilles to Narbonne, was seized by pirates and taken to North Africa and slavery for two years. Returned to his native France, he began his long life of labour for God and God's people.

His accomplishments, at the close of his 84 years of life, are the evidence of his sainthood. He grew steadily in the love of God, and in his holiness he became a faithful follower of the High Priest. But his love for his brothers and sisters in Christ grew apace with his love for God. Those of his contemporaries who were the beneficiaries of his charity were blessed indeed. Posterity is likewise indebted to him.

St. Vincent de Paul has justifiably come to be known as the Saint of Charity. He spent himself unstintingly in works of charity to alleviate the burdens of the poor, especially in the rural districts of France; to bring relief to prisoners and reform to the existing methods of dealing with prisoners, to harbour needy and abandoned children. His charity, however, was no mere philanthropy, devoid of God. Always he was primarily concerned with the souls of men. The Vincentian Fathers and the Sisters of Charity, whom we know so well because of their great work for God, owe their beginning to St. Vincent de Paul. The modern St. Vincent de Paul Society made up of laymen is but an extension of the saint's labours for the poor. In the present stained glass window the saint is shown with a little infant wrapped in his cloak, and about to take to the shelter of one of his houses a ragged little waif of the city. This is no mere fancy of the imagination, for the saint would often, especially in the quiet of night, wander the streets to pick up just-born infants, abandoned by their parents, and homeless children.

147

We note in the present window the outline of a church in the distance. It is the Cathedral of Notre Dame, of his beloved Paris. The medallion beneath the figure of St. Vincent de Paul depicts the Elder Tobias in the act of dispensing charity. He is known as one of the greatest of the Old Testament apostles of charity. Though his charity was limited to the people of his own race, who were suffering in captivity, nevertheless it was inspired by the love of the one true God. Tobias is the Old Testament counterpart of St. Vincent de Paul, apostle of Christ. The border for this is the fleur-de-lys, the national flower of France, and also, on either side the coat-of-arms of Pope Clement XII, who canonized St. Vincent de Paul.

> *The "Mother of Divine Grace" window is a gift in pious memory of Captain George Brown.*

> *The "St. Vincent de Paul" window is a gift in pious memory of Antone Connich. You are asked to remember them in your prayers.*

The Story of the "Passion" Window

The Theme

Almost the first lesson a Christian child is taught is of the love of the Son of God for men, the lesson of the Cross. Every single day thereafter, every time he signs himself with the sign of the Cross, he recalls the great act of man's Redemption. To omit the Crucifixion from the story of God and His people would be to omit the story itself. Prominent always in the mind of the Church and in the minds of the faithful is Calvary. Most fitting then is the theme of the new stained glass window in our parish church: the Passion of our Lord and Saviour, Jesus Christ.

Central Panel — The Crucifixion

The dominating scene in the window is that of the Crucifixion. *"It is consummated.' And bowing his head, he gave up the ghost."* The broken figure on the Cross is lifeless. It is the body of the Eternal Son of God, assumed just for this, the Crucifixion. His work is done. His task is finished. Heaven is at long last open to man. Behold here the depth of God's love for man in the sufferings and death of the Divine Son. At the foot of the Cross are the Mother of Jesus, the faithful apostle John, and the penitent sinner, Mary Magdalene.

Beneath the Crucifixion scene is the medallion depicting the Agony of our Lord in the Garden of Gethsemane. *"And there appeared to him an angel from heaven, strengthening him."* An angel from heaven comforts the beautiful figure of Christ, in unspeakable agony at the thought of His Passion and of untold sins and ungrateful sinners.

Left Panel — Old Testament

As in the "Christ the King" window, so in this "Passion" window the two side lancets are given over to scenes from the Old and New Testaments that have an intimate connection with the central theme. In the left panel are Old Testament scenes. The lowest medallion pictures the sacrifice of Abraham. An angel is staying the hand of the patriarch, who in obedience to God's command was about to sacrifice his only son, Isaac. The angel commends Abraham for his obedience to the difficult command, which God had given to test his faith and loyalty. *"Now I know thou fearest God and hast not spared thy only begotten son for my sake."* Abraham offering his only son Isaac is an accepted prefiguration of the Father consenting to the Crucifixion of His only begotten Son.

The middle medallion represents the first Passover. A Jewish family is represented carrying out the command given by God to the Jews in Egypt through their leader, Moses. The unblemished lamb, whose blood has been sprinkled on the doorpost, is being hastily eaten. Outside an angel may be seen, passing over the house, because of the sign upon the doorpost. *"And the blood shall be unto you for a sign."* The lamb, whose blood saved the Jews from bodily harm, is a definitely acknowledged type or figure of Christ, the *"Lamb of God,"* by whose blood all men are eternally saved. Or as the Church proclaims in her Easter Mass, *"Christ our true Pasch is immolated...He is the true lamb of God who takest away the sins of the world."*

The top medallion portrays an incident from the desert wanderings of the Jews. Beset by a plague of venomous serpents because of their rebellion against God, the Jews beg for relief from heaven. And the Lord said to Moses, *"Make a brazen serpent, and set it up for a sign: whosoever being struck shall look upon it, shall live."* In the present portrayal Moses stands beside the lifeless image, a live serpent crawls away, and a victim is being healed. For the connection between this Old Testament scene and the Passion we have only to consider Christ's own words, *"As Moses lifted up the serpent in the desert, so must the Son of man be lifted up."* *"And I, if I be lifted up from the earth, will draw all things to myself."*

Right Panel — New Testament

More familiar are the New Testament scenes in the right lancet. In the lowest the Blessed Mother and St. John keep their watch beneath the lifeless figure on the Cross. A Roman Centurion stands by the Cross. He has seen the sky become suddenly overcast. He has felt the earth tremble beneath his feet. And now he has just withdrawn his spear from the side of Christ, and has seen the last drops of blood and water flow from this final, useless wound. Suddenly he realizes and cries out his credo, *"Indeed this was the Son of God."*

In the center medallion is pictured a well-loved traditional scene: Joseph of Arimathea and Nicodemus take down the body from the Cross and lay it in the arms of the sorrowing Mother.

In the uppermost medallion is represented the burial. In a new tomb, hewn out of a rock, *"wherein no man yet has been laid,"* the disciples Joseph and Nicodemus place His sacred remains. To the very end His Mother and the beloved disciple keep their vigil.

The Rose Window

Surmounting all else is the Rose Window. Because of its symbolism it too carries the theme of the Passion. In the very center is the traditional figure of the Saviour, the Lamb. In the four opposite corners are adoring angels, offering their homage to the Saviour of mankind. In the oblique corners are the instruments of the Passion: the Cross, the hammer and nails, the sponge and spear, the crown of thorns.

This is the "Passion" window, a constant reminder of the love of Christ for men, and a spur to our own love for Him. "He hath borne our infirmities and carried our sorrows...He was bruised for our sins."

The Rose Window is a memorial gift in pious memory of Doctor Firmin Orella, Mr. Frank Kelly, and Mr. And Mrs. Joseph and Mathilde Schweitzer.

The Story of the Holy Eucharist Window, the Baptism Window, the Charity Window, and the Penance Window

The Holy Eucharist Window

The first window on the Epistle side of the nave of the church portrays the Institution of the Blessed Eucharist. The scene is the Last Supper, the First Mass. Christ is at table with His Apostles. On the morrow He will shed His blood for the remission of man's sins. On this eve of His Crucifixion He fulfills the promise which He had made, the promise which had so startled all and which had driven so many of the unbelieving away from Him. *"I am the living bread which came down from Heaven. If any man eat of this bread he will live forever; and the bread that I will give is My flesh for the life of the world."* Christ gives us Himself to be our food and drink in our journey through earth to Heaven. Mystery of Faith! Love of the Son of God for men! *"This is my body." "This is my blood."*

In the medallion of this window there is pictured Patriarch Moses and two women. The latter gather manna from the ground, the food which God sent miraculously each day from Heaven to refresh the Jews on their journey from Egypt to the Promised Land. Moses stands with grateful eyes fixed on Heaven, whence came the answer to his prayer for food for the people. The manna, like the multiplication of the loaves in the New Testament, is a type and shadow, destined to disappear in the full light of the Gospel dispensation. These things but prepare for the ineffable miracle of the Eucharist, the participation by Christians of Christ's Body and Blood. Our Savior, referring to this gift of Himself, said: "Your fathers did eat manna and are dead. He that eateth this bread shall live forever." It is interesting to note the figure of the Angel on either side of the border of the window. The angel holds a shield and upon the shield there is a chalice: *"the chalice of benediction which we bless, is it not the communion of the blood of Christ."*

The Baptism Window

On the Gospel side of the church the first window depicts the familiar scene of our Lord and Nicodemus, when the Divine Master insisted upon the necessity of Baptism for salvation. Nicodemus had come by night to hear our Lord. He tells him: *"unless a man be born again he cannot see the kingdom of God."* And to the query of Nicodemus how a man might be born again when he is old, our

Saviour gave answer: *"Unless a man be born again of water and the Holy Spirit, he cannot enter the kingdom of God."* This insistence of Our Lord on the necessity of Baptism is one of the clear evidences of the institution by Christ of the Sacrament of Baptism, the portal of the life of Sanctifying Grace. *"We are buried together with Him by baptism unto death; that as Christ is risen from the dead by the glory of the Father, so also we may walk in newness of life."*

The medallion beneath is a prefigurement of Baptism. In this small figure we see the noble Syrian, Naaman, washing himself in a river. Naaman had gone to the Prophet, Eliseus, seeking a cure from the dread disease of leprosy with which he was afflicted. Naaman, after some hesitation, obeyed and found to his joy and amazement that *"his flesh was restored like the flesh of a little child and he was made clean."* Sacred writers see here a prefiguring of the Sacrament of Baptism, for it is by the waters of Baptism that we are cleansed from the leprosy of sin. The angel in the border bears on the shield a lamp, the symbol of the gift of Faith, which we receive in the Sacrament of Baptism.

The Charity Window

The second window on the Epistle side of the nave of the church illustrates our Divine Lord's teaching of the virtue of Charity. This is the parable of the Good Samaritan. The despised citizen of Samaria bends over the beaten and bruised victim of robbers. He binds his wounds and prepares to care for him further. The Levite has passed by and curiously, but unconcerned, glances back. This is the story told by our Blessed Lord to teach all men the virtue of Charity, a necessary virtue of any follower of Christ. *"By this shall all men know that you are my disciples, if you have love one for another."* *"Go and do thou in like manner."*

The accompanying medallion depicts an Old Testament incident of Divine Charity. There was a famine in the land. At the command of God, the Prophet Elias went to Sarephta, a village over which the people of Sidon ruled. There he met a poor woman, a widow, who gave him of her want to assuage his hunger. And God then, through His Prophet, works a miracle of Charity for the poor, kind woman, even though she was not of the Chosen People. The pot of meal and her cruse of oil shall be used, but not spent. *"And from that day, the pot of meal wasted not, and the cruse of oil was not diminished, according to the word of the Lord, which He spoke in the hand of Elias."*

In the shield in the angel's hands, in the border of the window, is shown a flaming heart. A heart that is cold is a man that loves not: a heart that burns is a man in love with God and with his brothers and sisters in Christ.

The Penance Window

The second window on the Gospel side of the nave of the church teaches, through the story of the Prodigal Son, the Christian virtue of Penance. The young man had left his father's house and had gone, with his share of his inheritance, to enjoy himself in the world. He drank and played, and he came upon evil days, for the world loved him only as long as he had something to give it. And he suffered. Then came repentance, sorrow for his foolish ways and for his disregard of his father. He comes back and throws himself, in sincere sorrow, at his father's feet: *"Father, I have sinned against Heaven and before thee. I am not worthy to be called thy son."* And he was forgiven and taken back. Our Lord would teach us the indispensable virtue of Penance, for God loves the repentant sinner: *"There shall be joy before the angels of God upon one sinner doing penance."*

In the smaller scene below there is pictured the great act of repentance of David, the Royal Prophet. The Prophet Nathan has related to David the crime of a rich man who stole a poor man's only ewe to make a feast. David's anger was great, and he spoke: *"As the Lord liveth, the man that hath done this is the child of death."* Then Nathan pointed at David and cried: *"Thou are the man...Thou has killed Urias the Hethite with the sword and hath taken his wife."* And David fell on his knees in bitter sorrow: *"I have sinned against the Lord."*

In the border of this window the angel appears with broken chains upon the shield, a symbol of the effect of true repentance: the bonds of sin are broken, a soul is restored to the true Christian Life.

The Holy Eucharist Window is in pious memory of Mr. And Mrs. James Gilhuly. The Baptism Window is in holy memory of Lieutenant Charles Kendrich. The Charity Window is in pious memory of Mr. and Mrs. Pietro C. Rossi. The Penance Window is given by the Parish in memory of the young men of the Parish who lost their lives in World War II. You are asked to remember them in your prayers.

The Story of the Resurrection Window and of the Evangelist Windows

"If Christ has not risen, vain is your faith...But Christ has risen from the dead, the first fruits of those who have fallen asleep." The empty tomb is our Saviour's irrefutable, perennial answer to those who refuse to believe. It is the solid, constant foundation of Christian hope in an endless life the other side of the grave. It would be unthinkable that the triumph of Divinity, the Resurrection, should not find its proper place in the stained glass windows of our parish church.

The Resurrection Window

The Resurrection window pictures the graceful figure of the Risen Saviour. The inevitable triumph of Divinity. His right hand is raised in the benediction He is always so ready to impart. In His left hand He holds the banner of the Cross, now become a token of His Conquest. *"Death is swallowed up in victory. O death, where is thy victory? O death, where is thy sting?"* At the feet of the Risen Saviour cringe the soldiers, the guardians of the tomb. How futile are the arms of men to oppose the designs of God.

The medallion beneath depicts the scene from Sacred Scripture of Jonah and the whale. The significance of this incident is indicated by Christ Himself. *"Even as Jonah was in the belly of the fish three days and three nights, so will the Son of Man be three days and three nights in the heart of the earth."*

The border of this central window has three symbols which refer to the Divine Redeemer: The IHS, which are the first three letters of the Greek word for the name, Jesus; the AW, the first and last letters in the Greek Alphabet *"I am the Alpha and the Omega, the beginning and the end, who is and who was, and who is coming, the Almighty."* Finally, there is the Cross, the instrument by which Divinity would lead Humanity to eternal Heaven.

The St. John Window

The windows flanking the Resurrection portray the four Evangelists, the divinely inspired narrators of the life and teaching of Our Lord. It is in the oldest and truest tradition of Church art to so honor these great figures of apostolic times. To the immediate right of the Resurrection window is the window of the beloved St. John, Apostle and Evangelist. The Saint is shown with upraised glance, as though rapt in contemplation of the Divine Son in His heaven. The open book of his Gospel lies beside him. An eagle is at his feet, the ancient symbol of the main characteristic of this Evangelist: just as the eagle soars so high into the heavens, so St. John dwells continuously upon the Divinity of his Master.

The accompanying medallion represents the prophet Isaias. Like St. John, this great prophet sings in lyric fashion of the supernatural character of the Messiah, of whom he foretells so much. The scene portrayed depicts when Isaias, called by God to preach, protested his unworthiness, God sent an angel to touch with a burning, purifying coal the lips of His servant.

The St. Matthew Window

Just to the left of the Resurrection window is the window of St. Matthew, Apostle and Evangelist. This is the Apostle called from the profession of tax-gatherer to become God's gatherer of immortal souls. Noteworthy in the Gospel of St. Matthew is the ever-recurring insistence upon the fulfillment by Christ of the prophecies of the Old Testament. The Evangelist is seen standing with the book of his Gospel in his hand. At his side is the figure of a child with wings, the ancient symbol of this Saint.

The medallion below is of another of the great prophets of the Old Testament, Ezechiel. It was the mission of this prophet to keep alive, in the mind of the exiled Jews, their hope in the Messiah and His Kingdom. Ezechiel is seen here, with rays of light pouring down upon his head. *"The heavens were opened, and I saw the visions of God."*

The St. Luke Window

The other window at the Epistle side of the altar is that of St. Luke, Evangelist. Greek by birth. A physician by profession, St. Luke was a disciple of the great St. Paul. He must have been very close and very dear to the Blessed Mother, for he it is who tells so intimately of the Birth of the Saviour, and who speaks so lovingly of the Mother of the Divine Infant. The figure we see holds a scroll in his hand, suggesting his authorship of his Gospel. Beside him is the figure of an ox, the sacrificial animal of the Old Testament. The ox is always associated in ecclesiastical art with St. Luke, because of this sacred writer's constant reference to the Priesthood of Christ, whose sacrifice so infinitely surpassed the sacrifice of *"the blood of goats and bulls and the sprinkled ashes of the heifer."*

In the medallion of this window is shown the prophet Daniel and the startled, frightened king of Babylon, Baltasar. Daniel has just interpreted the mysterious writing, which had appeared on the wall of the king's palace: the dire sentence pronounced by God, the complete overthrow of Baltasar, because he had dared to drink with his guests from the sacred vessels of the Temple.

The St. Mark Window

Opposite the window of St. Luke is the window of St. Mark, Evangelist. The simple, concise Gospel of St. Mark lays great stress upon Christ, the Messiah, and upon the Messianic Kingdom. Beside the Saint, as he is shown here, is the traditional figure of a crouching lion, the king of the wild beasts. Christ, as St. Mark so constantly insists, is the Messiah, the Anointed One, the King of the only lasting Kingdom.

In the medallion is represented the fourth of the great prophets of the Old Testament, Jeremias. His great mission was to warn God's chosen people to hold fast, in captivity though they were, to the faith of their fathers. The prophet is here shown receiving upon his lips the touch of an angel's fingers, God's response to the cry of unworthiness of Jeremias.

The Borders of these Evangelist Windows contain certain very apt symbols. There is the Dove, a reminder that these men are inspired writers and that therefore, God is the principal author, and the mitre, symbolic of the episcopal office of the Evangelists. There is the symbol of cross and palm leaves: the Cross, symbolic of their martyrdom; the palm leaves, symbolic of their endless living with Him, whose life and teaching they wrote for all men.

The three center windows of the Resurrection Window are the kind gift of Mr. Joseph B. Keenan, in holy memory of his wife, Carlotta M. Keenan, and of his parents, Mr. and Mrs. Bernard R. Keenan. The window of St. Luke is in pious memory of Miss Jane Moran. The Window of St. Mark is in pious memory of Miss Anna Felchlin.

The Windows of the Saints

In the building of churches, Catholic tradition has always aimed at making everything in them recall vividly the reality of God, whose children we are. Art, music, ornamentation are used primarily to lift the mind in adoration to God, Who made all. Even the very structure of the edifice is designed to teach that here is God's dwelling place among men. So, too, the stained glass windows. They are fashioned to speak to us of God through the light that He has created.

The windows of St. Vincent de Paul parish church strive to carry on this holy tradition. The clerestory windows tell the story of God's dealing with His people. There are the great prophecies and foreshadowings of the Old Testament times, the long years of waiting for the Redeemer promised to the downcast Adam and Eve. We see the figures of the major prophets. More prominently we are shown the wondrous like of the Divine Saviour and King: the Incarnation, His Passion and Death, the Triumphant Resurrection. We are reminded of the Sacraments, the Divinely instituted channels of salvific Grace. The virtues the Master taught are brought before our eyes. The great evidences of the Divinity of Christ, His miracles, are pictured. We are shown the institution of the Spouse of Christ, His Church. And there are the figures of the Inspired Evangelists.

It is only fitting that a place should be found for some, at least, of the great saints of the Church, those historical figures whose lives were spent for the preservation of Christ's teachings. Some of the saints who have been chosen are unfortunately not too well known, except to those who have been privileged to study deeply the history of God's Church. But they are the outstanding teachers and defenders of the Faith – the Great Doctors of the Church.

First there are the windows inside the sanctuary. As is appropriate, the window by the Altar of the Virgin is dedicated to Mary. She is pictured with her mother, the good St. Anne. The daughter learns from her mother the wonders of Holy Writ, wherein was told of Him Who was to come, and Whom she would mother. Opposite, by his altar, is the window of St. Joseph, patron of the Universal Church. With Joseph is the Child Jesus. This window commemorates the old legend that the Son of God, as a young boy, used to help his foster-father at his carpentry.

In the body of the church come the windows of the saints. First on the Epistle side is the window of **St. Francis**, the beloved Poverello of Assisi (1226). It is he after whom our city is named. And he is a co-patron of the Archdiocese, hence his place in the church.

Next, in full Episcopal robes, stands the great Bishop of Alexandria, **St. Athanasius** (373). In an age not unlike our own, when people sought to question the claims of our Blessed Lord to Divinity, Athanasius stood as a great champion of Christ's cause.

Beside him is another of the outstanding Bishops of the time, **St. Basil** (378), called for his accomplishments, "the Great." He was Bishop of a province in what we know now as Asia Minor. Here he not only founded an Order of Monks and provided for the careful instruction of his people, but he became one of the principal defenders of the Faith against its adversaries.

On the Gospel side of the church we meet first the majestic figure of the great Apostle of Ireland, **St. Patrick** (493). He received his commission from Pope Celestine I to bring the faith to the pagan people of the little island. How well he succeeded is attested to by the great faith of the Irish people through the centuries.

With the beloved St. Francis of Assisi he is a co-patron of the Archdiocese, and for this reason finds a place in the church.

The last of the windows just installed represents **St. Gregory Nazianzen** (390), Patriarch of Constantinople. St. Gregory was a fellow student of St. Basil at the University of Athens. He became one of the greatest scholars of his time. His powers he devoted exclusively to good, to the defense of the Divinity of Christ, and to the zealous instruction of his flock in the things of God.

The group of windows lately installed brings to completion the installation of stained glass windows in St. Vincent de Paul Church. These newest windows complete the "Windows of the Saints." They enshrine still others of those particular Saints of the Church who are especially noted for handing down and preserving in its purity the teaching of our Divine Lord. These Saints are called Doctors of the Church, which means that they are acknowledged as the Church's greatest teachers. They have been outstanding as preachers and as teachers of that doctrine which we believe, and which came down to them, through the Apostles, from our Blessed Saviour. These Saints were even more. They were great public figures. They were conspicuous for their vigorous defense of Christian principles as the only answer to the burning questions of their times.

Of these latest windows, the first on the East side of the church presents **St. John Chrysostom**, Bishop of Constantinople. Distinguished as an orator (he was called by his contemporaries "Golden Tongue"), his talents were devoted to expounding the doctrine of the Divine Founder of the Church. His fearless denunciation of the moral and political corruption of contemporary civil authorities earned for him exile and, ultimately, death. Though written for the conditions of the fourth century, many of his works seem as if written for modern times.

Opposite him, on the West side, is **St. Augustine**, one of the greatest minds of all times. His zeal for the unadulterated teaching of his Divine Master has marked him as perhaps the foremost of all the Doctors of the Church. He, too, is remarkable as a public figure. During his lifetime he tried in vain to stop the wave of Barbarian hordes that swept through Europe and into his native Africa.

Next to St. Augustine and inextricably linked to him is the historic Bishop of Milan, **St. Ambrose**. It was his influence and persuasive argument that brought back to the Faith from which he had strayed the great Bishop of Hippo. His zeal for the careful instruction of his people is preserved in his simple and touching homilies, which have come down to us through the centuries.

On the East side of the church, facing St. Ambrose, is the well-known figure of **St. Thomas Aquinas**, the foremost theologian of the 13th century. St. Thomas

Aquinas rivals St. Augustine for the title of greatest of all the Doctors of the Church. His accurate presentation of our Divine Lord's teaching has clearly established that all Christian Doctrine is in perfect harmony with human nature, which God has given us. Today his works are still in use. They give us the most balanced and rational of all philosophies.

Beside him stands **St. Jerome**, robed in Cardinal's attire. In art he traditionally appears as a Cardinal of Rome. To his untiring and careful scholarship is due the translation of the Sacred Scriptures from the original Hebrew. As a man of his own times he took an active part in writing against those who tried to teach false doctrines. He was likewise strong in his denunciation of moral laxity in his era.

The last window on the East side is devoted to **St. Teresa** of Avila in Spain, one of the most remarkable women Saints of the Church. The 16th century, so fruitful of religious rebellion, found her able to accomplish many needed reforms in the Church. Her spiritual writings have been so exceptional that she has been accorded the title of Doctor of the Church.

Another woman Saint, one of a family of 23 children, **St. Catherine** of Siena in Italy, is found in the last window of the West side of the church. Her writings are a clear exposition of the Christian way of perfection for every follower of her Divine Master. Though a mystic, she was instrumental in making it possible for the Papacy of the 14th century to resume residence in Rome, from which the violence of that age had forced it.

In the vestibule of the church are found representations of two of the most popular of modern devotions. In the East window is depicted the revelation of the Sacred Heart to **St. Margaret Mary Alacoque**. On the West side is the window of Lourdes, the representation of the vision of our Blessed Lady to **St. Bernadette**.

Of the clerestory windows, that of the Risen Christ and St. Thomas has been given by Mr. Vincent Arrillaga in commemoration of his son Francis. That of the Transfiguration is donated by Mrs. Andrew Brannigan, commemorating her husband Mr. Andrew Brannigan.

The window portraying the Miracle of Cana is the gift of Mr. and Mrs. Andrew Lynch in sacred memory of Mrs. Helen O'Neill. The window depicting the Cure of the Paralytic is given by Mrs. Rinaldo Sciaroni in pious memory of her mother Mrs. Francis Green.

In the lower tier the window of our Blessed Mother and St. Anne is the gift of our Blessed Mother's Sodality of the Parish. That of St. Joseph is donated by the Ushers' Club of the Parish. Those of St. Francis and St. Athanasius are given by Mrs. Virgil John Oliva in pious memory respectively of her parents Mr. and Mrs. Antone and Mary Jane Marengo and of her husband Mr. Virgil John Oliva.

The St. Patrick window is the gift of the Kenny family in sacred memory of their parents, Patrick and Ellen Kenny. The St. Gregory window is the generous gift of Mrs. George F. Brown. The St. Basil window is the gift of Mrs. G. Golden and Mrs. F. Maionchi in holy memory of their father Domenico Balanesi.

The St. Augustine window has been given in pious memory of Michael Gnecco and of Charles and Elizabeth Davis. The St Ambrose window is in holy remembrance of Joseph Vannoni. The window honoring St. John Chrysostom is the gift of a family of the parish.

The St. Jerome window is in holy memory of the deceased members of the Raisch and Remer families. The window dedicated to St. Teresa of Avila is the generous gift of the Gehm family. The window dedicated to St. Catherine of Siena is in pious remembrance of Catherine Vernazza.

The window of the Sacred Heart is in sacred remembrance of Anna Armanini and Edith Sagiacomo. The window of Our Lady of Lourdes is in sacred memory of Pestonjee Davar.

The generosity of the donors of these windows has made it possible to add the final touch to the beauty of the church. The richness of color, the delicate artistry, and the wealth of illustration from the Sacred Scriptures of our Divine Lord's life and teaching have blended together wonderfully in the stained glass windows of the church. *"I have loved the beauty of Thy house and the place where Thy glory dwelleth."*

Memories of the Earthquake of October 17, 1989

Reverend John K. Ring

Pastor

St. Vincent de Paul Church

MEMORIES OF THE EARTHQUAKE OF OCTOBER 17, 1989

REVEREND JOHN K. RING
PASTOR
ST. VINCENT DE PAUL CHURCH

It was a warm autumn day, a day in which San Francisco is at its best - to look at, to walk through, to live in, and to enjoy the City and its people.

As school was getting out for the day I greeted the parents and said good-bye to the children. I then walked down to the bank on Lombard and then to one on Chestnut to have a document notarized for the estate of my mother who had died September 4th. To get a change of pace from a hard and busy day, I walked down through the Marina. Many people were out like myself. I remember remarking to someone how pleasant it was to be able to be out and meet so many parishioners as I walked. After a good walk and many conversations, I headed up Steiner Street. I was stopped by John Puccinelli by the grocery store on Greenwich. We had a good chat. We were joined by the grocer. He insisted I have a cup of his special Italian coffee. I did. Sandie Tucker, our school secretary came along. We all chatted. Then I made my way up Steiner, made a visit to the church, closed the church, and went to my room. I was hot. I took off my shirt. My private phone rang. It was my brother, the Pastor of St. Timothy's in San Mateo. I sat down in my desk chair to talk. Mid-sentence he didn't make sense. He blurted: "It's shaking...the earth...everything is shaking...the glass it's all falling...I'm getting..." And then it hit me from behind; it felt as if a car ran into my lower back. The glass and the shutters were shaking. The room and the chandelier were moving. I moved around the desk, still holding the phone. I shouted to Vin on the phone. There was no one there. I dropped the phone. I had to so I could hold onto the end of the desk and green chair so I wouldn't fall over. The house was like a noisy bucking bronco. Then I heard the child-care students screaming in the school yard. I threw on a shirt as I ran down the stairs - I remember hearing glass breaking and seeing the hallway chandeliers swinging wildly as I ran. The two teachers, Debbie and Theresa, had all the children huddled around them in the center of Green Street. Debbie was concerned whether that was the best place because of the wires. Looking at the buildings all around us, I said there was no other place. We'd have to trust the wires. The principal, George Enes, and Father O'Neil quickly joined us. Five very frightened adults trying to calm the fears of the children. The children were good. Slowly we brought them back to the safety of the sidewalk.

I went by myself to check the church. Going through the rectory to get there, I met Mrs. Matteucci, our cook; she was her usual calm self. She showed me the statue of Our Lady in one of the, offices. It had fallen over. Half of the moon under her feet had broken off.

I could see that all of the pictures on the rectory walls were at different angles and the plaster on the wall of the staircase to the second floor had cracked and some had fallen. With fear at what I would find, I entered the church. The first thing I noted was that the sanctuary candle was out; the wax had moved so much that it extinguished the flame. The left candlestick at Mary's altar was down. The gates of the altar rail had swung to an almost closed position. There were pieces of plaster and chips of paint all over the church. Over all the arches there were cracks running horizontally, also under the windows on the west side. In the sanctuary there were vertical cracks along the seams. All the Stations of the Cross were at different angles; many of the nails that were meant to hold them in place had popped out; fortunately the hooks held. Amazingly – what I had worried about the most – all the magnificent stained glass windows were intact. In fear and in humility and in gratitude, I knelt before the Lord. I prayed. I looked upon Him on the cross. He was nailed there. In His time of abandonment and fear He could not run. An earthquake did not offer to Him just the possibility of death, it was the sign of His death. I prayed for my parishioners. I prayed for my family. I prayed in gratitude that Mom had died six weeks ago. She didn't like earthquakes; this would have really frightened her. And her death saved me a frightening decision: to go to see how she was or to go check on how my parishioners were. I could no longer be alone. I had to be with the people. I went out to the corner of Green and Steiner. Debbie Rivard came, she had driven home to check on her place. She said that all the streets in the Marina were up-ended and houses falling and there was a fire. Seeing that everything I could see looked okay I dismissed her description as hysteria. Young Tom Leonardini came speeding up on his bike. He said there was confusion all over, and there was a fire. My cousin Matt Ward came running up. He had been remodelling a house up on Green and Fillmore. He was on his way home across the Golden Gate Bridge. He turned around and came back to check on the safety of the lady he was working for and the safety of the house – then he checked on me. As Tom and Matt and I talked, Celine Curran pulled up. She had her mother Mae Watters (she had retired as church secretary just the day before) in the car, she was taking her home. Celine said that she had heard that the tower at St. Dominic's had fallen and one wall of the church was down – a number of people stopped to ask how our church was.

I went into the rectory. I told Mrs. Matteucci that I'd eat later when I had time. I had to get down to the people in the Marina. I went up to my room to put on my clerics and to get the Holy Oils. I was relieved to see my room. All the pictures were at different angles. In my living room, one piece of Belleek had fallen and broken. The tall Lladro figures of the Madonna and the two nuns had fallen face down, but remained on their shelf undamaged. The small wooden statues in the curio cabinet had toppled, but all the Waterford was safe. In my office, the wooden statue of St. Vincent de Paul and its marble pedestal had fallen over. No damage. One vase had fallen from the circular book case - cracked but not broken. The ceramic figures had moved to the edge but did not fall. I went up to my upper room - the Crow's Nest from which I could see most of the parish plus the Bay and Marina. I noted that two candlesticks and two statues had fallen over, also a couple vases. A picture of the Acropolis had fallen, its glass shattered. Then I saw what I had come up there to see - the Marina. Yes, there was a fire - a very large fire. Was the whole Marina going to burn? I left quickly.

I met the principal outside. He had studied all the school structures. He led me on a quick tour of all the major damage. Fortunately it was what appeared to be only plaster off the horizontal beams in his outer office and the 1st grade and in the health room and computer room and library (plus most of the books there were on the floor as well as the globe of the world). A lot of other cracks plus all the statues of Mary fell off their corner platforms plus the figure of the Viking, after which our sports' teams are called. I told George that there was definitely no school tomorrow and that I'd somehow talk to him about a decision for future days. He said he would come in the morning anyway to talk to any who came and be sure they were provided for. I left for the Marina.

Down through Cow Hollow to Chestnut, people were out talking nervously. A great number were, from the higher spots or from roof tops, watching the fire in the Marina. The flames and the smoke were frightening even from Pierce Street as I crossed Lombard. There were no street lights working there and drivers were moving slowly and politely. One driver stopped and asked for more prayers from me.

Once I got to Chestnut I began to see the real damage. I zig-zagged my way through the Marina. I met startled strangers. I embraced well known parishioners. I hugged frightened children. I was fully aware of the smell of gas everywhere, and the deeper I got into the area, the stronger it became. I met a parishioner standing under his cock-eyed garage door. He said that every doorway in his home was the same way. I met a woman walking in a daze saying she lost her Hummel collection and all her crystal. I met people packing up their cars. I met others already fleeing. I walked up a slab of sidewalk and down the next slab. I saw five foot utility boxes lifted in the sidewalk and lying there like abandoned coffins. I walked along sidewalks that were now sloped to the street. I stepped over cracks in the street I saw thirty-unit apartment houses leaning out over the street. All of their garage doors sprung open at different angles. At one corner I saw a pile of brick; it had been the facade of the building. And I saw faces and I heard words and I spoke words to those faces.

And then I saw the apartment house on Beach; it seemed to be kneeling on the street, its lower two stories tucked under its still stately third floor. It was resting on a few cars. Its windows were open for viewing. But you could not look because the fire was overwhelming. The whole apartment at Beach and Divisadero was engulfed in furious flames. I walked among the hoses and firemen - looking for people and for victims. All the emergency personnel were most accepting of my presence. The victims I saw were all living - people who had escaped with only what they were wearing. They were grateful and they were sad. They were watching their history burn. I watched all the young people, their "yuppie" image discarded as they volunteered to help hold the firehoses. I watched a whole string of them quickly move as one unit to redirect the water. The flames had suddenly begun to jump Beach Street and lick the apartment house on the south-west corner. Their speed was effective; the flames retreated. I remember a fireman on an aerial ladder hosing the fire, the light of the fire silhouetting him with the Palace of Fine Arts as the backdrop. I remember a policeman asking me if I knew some man with a French name. He and his crippled wife lived in that apartment house. He was at the store when the quake hit and the fire started. He had not been seen since. The policeman wanted to inform him that someone had rescued the wife and she was being sent to the hospital for safety. I did not know them. I remember being interviewed by some radio station. I was surprised later to learn how much I had said. I was too busy then to pay attention or remember. I was grateful to learn from some parishioner that later, in the middle of the night, she was alone and scared in the darkness of her home listening for news on her transistor radio - and she heard my voice and my words in that interview and she was so happy to hear I was alive, and that fact brought her the comfort she then needed (I was surprised at how many people I knew heard that interview. That was all they could learn of me for days because we were without a phone and even after service was restored because I was rarely at home.)

I tried to get down Divisadero to Jefferson to see if I could find our parish receptionist Juanita Arfsten. She had left work only ten minutes before the quake. Because of the fire and the fallen building I could not. A burly parishioner came running to me sobbing. He dissolved in my arms. His house was next to the fallen one, it was leaning on his. He and his sons had immediately gotten wrenches and gone around turning off the gas on their side of the street - but already the flames had prevented them from crossing the street to the apartment house and the adjoining flats, the home of one of our school families. It too was now engulfed in flames. And their neighbor was crying for them as well as for his own family.

I met people. Some I knew. Some I didn't. I said that, if they had no place to go, they should come to St. Vincent de Paul. We had no lights. We had no gas. We had no phone. But we had a roof. I met ones with transistor radios. I learned there had been damage to the Bay Bridge and on freeways. I met people that had been at the World Series game at Candlestick Park. They had walked and thumbed rides. Some said people were carrying away parts of the upper deck. I thought it was wrecked. I met a young women speeding up on roller skates. She lived on Russian Hill and came the fastest way possible when she saw where the fire was. She was looking for her family. I took her to her father. He was the burly man who was sobbing. I met one of our people, who had just celebrated his 90th birthday. He was standing in the street speechless. His wife came. She said that the earthquake had thrown her down the stairs. She was concerned for him. He was disoriented by the quake. I told them that they were to come to the rectory. I'd give them a bed. It was a ray of hope for them.

Someone told me the Red Cross was trying to see if they could set up the Marina Middle School as a shelter. I went there to see if it were true and if St. Vincent de Paul's buildings could be of any help. The Red Cross was there. I was directed to the one in charge - I believe his name was Bob Kirby - he was calm and in control. He appreciated the offer - said they were having trouble with the emergency generator there - they might need help - took all the information - asked my immediate plans - when I said I was running back to the rectory for a minute - he asked if he could reach me there - I said only if he could shout because there was no phone - and without power no doorbell. I said I would come back to check on the need. If he needed me sooner, send a police car.

No trouble crossing Lombard. Drivers were cautious. Everything was in darkness. The rectory was in blackness.

No one was home. Father Legaspi was on his day off. Father O'Neil must be out in the streets. I was starved. It was after nine o'clock. I hadn't eaten since noon - A shout came from the parking lot. A light shone in the kitchen window. It was the school secretary. She wanted to know if we were okay. She said her phone was working. I said I'd like to call my sister and brother. On the way to her place, Sandie turned off the gas to the church and school and rectory. I knew where the box was, but she knew what to do. We couldn't get the lid off the one at the convent. I couldn't reach either my sister or my brother. Sandie said she'd keep trying during the night. I went back to the rectory for dinner.

There was no light at all as after a bite of dinner I walked back down Steiner Street. There were no cars on the streets. I was in the darkness in the center of Steiner and Union - and a voice shouted: "Father Ring." I froze and then moved to the voice on the bench by the Church of St. Mary the Virgin. It was the woman and the 90 year old man that I had met earlier. There were young people with them. They had come up to the rectory to stay, but nobody answered the door when they rang and knocked so they were going to try to find someplace else to stay. I took them back to the rectory. They too had not eaten - so I got them milk and crackers and whatever food they wanted. I said I had to go back to the Middle School so I left them sitting there in the candlelight of the kitchen. They said they were too upset to go to bed yet.

I made it back to the Middle School. They were getting organized. The generator was working. Cots were being set up in the gym. People were already beginning to claim their own. The man in charge said that so far they were coping, that they did not need our buildings yet. I saw the large group of people still waiting to be assigned cots - I went up to the gym to talk to those already settled - so many of them I knew, most of them were widows and spinsters, one a woman and her older son. I don't remember any children. So many very proper and elegant older people, suddenly homeless - I told a number of them that, if they wished a long time solution, I'd open the convent for them. All they had to do is take the veil, and we'd have a newly created community! Seriously I said it was theirs to use. I mingled among the ones not yet settled. I offered the rectory to some but they said they'd stay with all their neighbors at the school. I looked for our parish receptionist and her daughter. I could not find them. I found one of our lectors; she was relieved to be able to come with me. I met one of our older parish leaders. She said that she talked to her son 15 minutes before the quake - and, though they lived only blocks apart, she had been walking the streets ever since and could not find him. She was rising to come with me when in walked her son and his wife - a good time for a reunion.

At the rectory I found that two young neighbors of the elderly couple had joined them for food and shelter. There would be seven of us there that night. I settled them into the old housekeeper's room and the rooms on the third floor. I left. I went down to see if the school secretary had reached my family. She hadn't reached my brother. She had talked to my sister. I was then able to reach her. Vin had just talked to her so now we knew that we were all safe. I dragged myself back up the hill, then decided that, as Dean, I should check on St. Dominic's. Even help this late might be appreciated. I drove up and parked at California to avoid all the expected debris. There was none. The tower and the wall were still standing. The streets were blocked because, as some of the Dominicans told me, some pieces had fallen on the southern side. They had been inside singing Vespers. One priest found himself hiding under the pulpit with Matthew, Mark, Luke, and John. As I drove back, I could see the fire still smoldering in the Marina, but all else was darkness.

It was well after midnight. I was exhausted physically and even more so emotionally. As I was about to put out the candle, my private phone rang! It was Dan Piro, a long-time friend. How great it was to hear the voice of a friend. After caring for so many during the past seven hours, it was comforting to hear someone caring about me. Selfish? True. We talked a long time. I needed it. As soon as I hung up, it rang again. It was Dan Murphy, a cousin. They were okay. He had gone to check on Mom's house. It was okay. Only one lamp had fallen - the one next to her bed; it had fallen away from there and hit the wall.

At last to bed, but every after-shock awakened me.

Early Wednesday morning I checked the church again by flashlight and decided to open it for Mass. It was still dark so I set many candles around the altar. More people came than usual, but not as many as I expected, but how could they? They had moved or were in shelters! It was an emotional Mass mingling gratitude and sorrow, fear and wonder. I commented in my homily that, as we began the Mass in the morning's darkness and would conclude it in the light of the sun, so we as a people of hope and faith would be able to move from the darkness of yesterday into the light of all the tomorrows.

I greeted all of our houseguests and offered them breakfast. One said she wanted only toast. I asked how without electricity. Juice and cold pastries and milk weren't that bad. I joined the principal and the vice-principal and the secretary in the school yard. Only one child came to school expecting it to be open (Only one can have a perfect

170

attendance record this year!) Some school families came to
check on the school to see if there was anything they could
do to help. One of the men was a contractor so he came and
looked at the church for me and said that he too did not think
the cracks offered any danger. The principal wondered what
to tell the faculty and the parents about school for tomorrow.
I said that the news for the public schools would be better
publicized than ours so they should be told that we would
follow whatever Mr. Cortines the Superintendent of Public
Schools announced for the city schools.

I knew people would need us today, but how could they
reach us? I put a clipboard and paper and pen outside the
rectory door with the note stating that both the phone and the
doorbell were not working so, if they needed us and could not
find us, they were to leave their name and where we could find
them. A wise move. Many offers of help. Some need for help.
A funeral postponed for Thursday. A funeral requested for
Friday. I greeted the people arriving and leaving the 9:15
a.m. Mass. Yes, we had been fortunate - Robert Waal the son
of parishioners and a graduate of our school came. He was a
civil engineer. He went through the rectory. It was the size
of building he was qualified to comment on. He was pleased
with the structure. We went down to the foundations. The
building had held, but he said that we should have it bolted
to the foundation and the cross beams strengthened by "T
bars". He went through the church and all of its foundations.
Quite impressed with all the retrofitting that Father O'Kane
had done after the '57 quake (did he save us this time?) He
was concerned about some of the cracks upstairs and the west
wall seeming to be out of plumb - but said he was not
qualified for so large a structure. This is his report:

St. Vincent de Paul Church

A preliminary inspection of the church foundation and lower
chapel shows very minor damage from the earthquake. Only
apparent distress are a few cracks in the plaster around the
column supports of the north end. Findings in the main church:

Many major plaster cracks are noticeable all throughout the
church. On the West end of the altar is a plaster crack
that has pushed out about 3/8" from the wall. The West
wall in the first half of the church may appear to have a
bulge point half way up and the wall is slightly out of
plumb. My recommendation is to have someone familiar with
the structure of the church to inspect the damage for
further recommendations.

Robert C. Waal, P.E.

A preliminary check of the walls and the foundation shows the structure in satisfactory condition. The only signs of distress to be found are the walls along the stairwells. Apparently most of the cracks are from previous settlement. I would recommend in the future that the foundation is properly connected to the walls. i.e. no foundation bolts are visible. A bracing system on the post and beam foundation that supports the middle floors should be installed.

Robert C. Waal, P.E.

I then went down to the Marina again. The same walk I had done yesterday afternoon before the quake. It was another beautiful day, but it was a totally different neighborhood. All the cracks and the gaps were startling. The upended sidewalks and the uneven streets. All the leaning buildings and the fallen ones. All the doors and the windows that were popped open. The gas meter covers with holes blown out of them. The sand in the streets. The sunken driveways. The toppled arterial signs. Buildings in the center of blocks still standing and stately ones at the ends crooked and without stairs. People welcoming me. People thanking me for being with them. People concerned about the church, especially about the stained glass windows. People staring, people moving, people gawking, people photographing. The press all over. Very friendly and polite. I remember being interviewed by about eight at once - one from Germany, one from Canada, one from the New York Times, one from Kansas City, from all over. They had been here for the World Series and told to cross the city and get stories. They were used to writing about sports. I said I felt sorry for them because, unlike me, they were not used to earthquakes and now they had experienced one and had to write about it. I said a lot of other things as I later read in some of the articles published around the world. I met one reporter from San Diego. I told him that he was here and our Archbishop was there at the bishops' meeting and gave him a bit of trivia for his article: The Archbishop was also out of the City in 1906, he was in Chicago. Later that day I met one reporter for the London Times. When they got news there of the quake, he was put on a plane immediately and told to fly the ten hours to cover it. I told him I had flown that same route two months before on August 12th and we had hit terrible turbulence an hour out of London. I was more scared then than I was by the earthquake! In the course of my wanderings that morning I met many people among them Joseph Alioto, the former mayor and his wife. In the midst of our conversation we were interrupted by a reporter from the Chronicle. He ignored me and wanted to talk to the mayor. Very kindly the mayor said he should be talking to me because I was the Pastor of St. Vincent de Paul Church and I and the Church had been doing so much for all the people of the area since it happened. He gave us more praise than we deserved. Most gracious of him and a learning lesson for the reporter and for me.

I needed to get to the Marina Middle School. As I started there some men approached and said they were evacuating their 93 year old mother. They had come back for some of her possessions while she waited in their van a few blocks away. Would I go and talk to her and bless her. I did but we could not talk. She spoke only Italian. I went over Francisco Street carefully because the streets and sidewalks were badly damaged. There was a strong smell of gas on that street. I saw a parishioner sitting in the sun in her driveway. I told her to leave, there was too much gas around. She said she had been told it was safe. I told the policeman at the corner and the PG&E man at the next one. I didn't want to be the only one worrying. The Middle School operation was in full motion. A lot of volunteers. A lot of food coming in. A lot of people and a lot of activity. One particularly bothersome parishioner saw me and grabbed her suitcase and my arm and said she was coming to stay with me. I quickly thought: if I have her at the rectory, I'll have to take care of her all the time and won't be able to care for anyone else. So I gently told her to put down her suitcase for now, that I have some decisions to make, and that I'd be back later. My normal stall. I talked to the staff of the Red Cross again. They said they could house 550, not beyond. I said that I'd be back.

I made my way back to the rectory. As I crossed Union Street, I spotted the daughter of our receptionist in a food line at the sandwich shop and there was her mother sitting at the table inside the window and she was weeping. I went in to console her. They had driven around part of the night. They couldn't go into their place. They then went to a friend, but she was being evacuated too. I commanded them to move to the rectory until there was another solution.

I checked my clipboard at the door. A lot of messages but not one word that anyone from the Chancery Office or Catholic Charities or Catholic Social Service had been by to check on us or offer help. I decided it was my responsibility then to report to them on the condition of the people of the parish. I phoned the Chancery Office and got the answering machine. Someone had gone in long enough to record that the office was closed and if there was major damage to any building... I hung up. No mention of people. I phoned the Archbishop's private number. No answer. I phoned the house number and Father Bruce Dreier answered. It was good to talk to him and to leave a message for the Archbishop that we and almost all of our people survived.

I finally reached my brother in San Mateo. We were astonished to come to know that he had sustained far more parish and personal damage than I had. He lost the statues of the Blessed Mother and St. Joseph in the church plus most of his Waterford and Belleek and Lladro and his Seated Cardinal. His curio cabinet had fallen over. As it did, its door popped open and dumped everything out. The door did not break, nor its side glass. Only one shelf broke plus everything in it including the old black-label Belleek plate that Mom had willed to him.

I called a staff meeting with Father Legaspi and Father O'Neil. We shared our information and our reactions. I asked that the three of us keep up a high visibility, always in Roman Collar. The Church had to be visible and apparently we were the Church. There was no sign of anyone else. We also discussed people living in the rectory. No problem. We discussed housing people in the gym and the school. It was agreed upon that our facilities would be available to everyone but only after Marina Middle School was filled. I said that we would have to depend on the Red Cross to get light, cots, food and volunteers. If we were to open up before they were filled down there, we would not be serving a need. In fact, we would be hampering their effort by causing them to split their attention between two different locations. It would be better to concentrate and do it well there. Our place would be available to them when needed and we priests would be available and visible as much as we could. I went back down to talk to the Red Cross. The ones I talked to agreed with our plan. I mingled with the people, ate some of the food they were beginning to serve for dinner and had a lot of juice. (I was amazed at how thirsty I was during all of these days. I was grateful for all the juices served there as well as the cans of water from Anheuser Busch.) As I returned to the rectory the two other priests were on their way to visit at the shelter - they returned sometime later. We picked at food in the refrigerator. There was no way to cook. All three of us then returned to be with the people and see that they were safe for the night. How impressed we were by all the young people who had volunteered and were there with the elderly talking to them and consoling them and being like grandchildren to them.

We returned to the rectory extremely tired about ten o'clock. There would be only six staying there tonight. The others had gone to relatives. I phoned the principal to say that I had heard the public school superintendent was reopening the schools. I said to spread the word that, due to the devastation and confusion in our area, our school would not reopen until Monday no matter what any superintendent of schools said. The principal agreed.

Then there was commotion in the house. I heard Father
O'Neil go down the stairs, I heard voices at the front door
and in the vestibule. I hung up and went to see. Who was
standing in the hallway but Archbishop Quinn and Bishop
Sevilla and poor Father O'Neil in his bathrobe! What had
happened was that the Archbishop had tried ringing the
doorbell, had seen candlelight in my office and shouted and
shouted, then moved around to the parking lot and shouted some
more. Father O'Neil heard. He heard a voice calling:
"Father Ring! Father Ring!" He opened the window and the
voice said: "I'm here to see Father Ring. This is the
Archbishop." Bishop Sevilla recognized Father O'Neil and
verified that it was the Archbishop. They had come, as soon
as they could after returning from San Diego, to see how we
were. I led them upstairs by flashlight to my room. Father
O'Neil went off to bed. Father Legaspi had not heard
anything. We needed more light so I lit the candle on the
credenza. I told the bishops that it was a most appropriate
candle to light on this night in their presence. I had just
found it among my mother's memories. It was the candle I had
carried into St. Mary's Cathedral on June 10, 1961. The last
time it had been lighted was at my Ordination as I said
"Adsum" to the Bishop's call. They listened to my report and
my stories. As usual, I managed to put my foot in my mouth.
I said, "All the arches..." and stopped and said that I
couldn't finish the sentence without getting in trouble, but
it was true: "all the church's arches are cracked". The
Archbishop laughed and said he would try not to take it
personally and then quoted someone as saying it's good to be
cracked because you're letting light in. The Archbishop said
that he wanted to come to offer Mass with us. We agreed on
Friday at 9:15 a.m. I led them by candlelight out to their
car in the darkness outside. I deeply appreciated their visit
and their concern.

Thursday life was a bit more normal. Again, the Mass was
moving by candlelight. Today no children came to school.
The staff returned to work. People came to offer their help.
One of the people startled me by even offering to do our
laundry. How practical. I was so startled, I said no. Later
one of the teachers asked if she could do anything and I said
yes and gave her my laundry. Her turn to be startled! A
woman from St. Dominic's came to say that she had gas and
electricity and she'd be happy to cook a meal for someone.
I asked if the someone could be priests! Rather than have her
buy any food or before it would turn bad in the defrosting
freezer, I gave her a turkey and a prime rib from our freezer.
She wondered how I could be so trusting as to give such food
to a stranger. I said "as easily as a stranger was offering
to cook the same food for us to eat." That food was to save
us

in the four days we were without gas with which to cook. Reece Miller and another man came in response to my call to American Building Maintenance to take down the Stations of the Cross before they fell. They spent the day doing it. They had to use a pulley. Each one weighs over a hundred pounds. How fortunate that no one was ever killed by one. They will not hang again in my time as Pastor. The lighter ones from the Chapel will replace them. A lot of people arrived for the postponed funeral; that doesn't happen too often. The widow was afraid to come back to the city so soon after the quake.

I told the receptionist Juanita Arfsten and the secretary Christine Martino to disturb me only if it were urgent. (I had found a rather large and loud brass bell to be the intercom.) I had to write a letter to the people of the parish. I wanted it to be mailed to every home. I wanted it in Sunday's bulletin. I wrote:

The Church of
St. Vincent de Paul
2320 Green Street
San Francisco, California
94123-4625

Dear Parishioners of St. Vincent de Paul,

May the God of all consolation give to each of you the comfort and the strength that you need in this time of sorrow and of stress. May the peace of Christ our Saviour return to your hearts and minds. May His Spirit give you new life and new hope.

Our buildings shook and some of them fell, but our faith is strong and unfaulting. Some lost many material possessions and some of us only a few, but all of us kept those possessions that are really valuable: faith, hope, and love. All of us wondered how we would survive, and we did and for this in humble gratitude we fell on our knees and say thanks to God.

But we cannot remain on our knees because there is work to be done. Our neighbors continue to be in need so each one of us must busy ourselves in helping one another. And this you have been doing so marvelously. I congratulate you on your love and concern for one another. As, on the evening of the earthquake and the days following, I made my way up and down your streets and met with you at your homes or at the community shelter at Marina Middle School. I marvelled at your compassion and care for one another and your faith-filled optimism. As I, with Father Legaspi and Father O'Neil reached out to you, we were touched by the ways you reached out to us. We are grateful to you and to Archbishop Quinn who, as soon as he could, came over to visit and check on the welfare of our parish and then returned on Friday to offer Mass with us for the intentions of all of you. In a special way in this Mass we prayed in thanksgiving for the services of the Red Cross and the Fire and Police Departments as well as the medical services and the PG&E and telephone workers and all the enthusiastic volunteers who served our community in need. May God bless them all.

We grieve for those who died. We offer sympathy for those who survived. We are saddened for those who lost homes and possessions. At the same time, we rejoice that we continue to live and continue to be strong enough to serve one another.

I have just had our Church buildings quickly studied for safety and for soundness. Yes, those are cracks you see as well as chipped paint and plaster, but underneath the foundations are apparently strong and solid. I am sure that the same is true of each one of us. We are showing cracks, we are a bit chipped by the stress and the strain of these days, but, thanks be to God, underneath we are finding solidity and strength in our faith and in our hope and in our love of God and our loving concern for one another. And in this fact we find peace and life and consolation.

Faithfully yours in Christ,

Reverend John Kevin Ring
Pastor

JKR:cm

177

It is written. Now it's up to the poor staff to prepare the mailing. It can go with the All Souls letter and envelope that is supposed to go next week.

The couple for Saturday's wedding is in. Is the church okay for a wedding? If there is still no electricity, there will be no lights and no organ. Thank God for candles and a piano.

Off to see the people in the Marina and at the shelter. How encouraging to see the great number of people. But it is sad: they are finding out if their place is red-tagged (no entry) or yellow-tagged (15 minutes to get necessary items) or green-tagged (free to return to). A confusing process to find out bad news. At least they were thoughtful enough to have an "express line" for the elderly. A few parishioners were happy to accept the title of "elderly" in order to find out quickly. Over at the cafeteria, people are already eating. The "nuns" and the "priests" from the Holy Order of Man are there serving. Someone congratulated me on the presence of the Church. I gulped and kept walking. Several times over the days I was asked where the Church was. I had to say honestly that I knew where St. Vincent de Paul Church was and they were seeing us often and everywhere. As to the rest, I had no idea.

But, when I did return to the rectory there was a message on the clip board that said that at 5:00 p.m. Thursday the head of Catholic Social Service and the representative for the homelessness from the Mayor's Office had stopped by to see if they could help in any way with the displaced. "Call the mayor's office first". All I could say when I did call Catholic Social Services was: "Where were you for 48 hours?" As I said to others: With the exception of Archbishop Quinn, the Roman Catholic Church could not have kept a lower profile if it had hired a couple of professionals to coordinate it. What a great disaster plan! In the future, I hope our only disaster plan is to dial 911 and find out the number of the Red Cross. Otherwise we're wasting our time and raising our expectations foolishly.

The wedding party arrived for the rehearsal for Saturday's wedding. Father O'Neil was taking charge of it. Just as they were about to begin, the lights came back on. It looked good after 48 hours without it. The first doorbell to ring brought CBS and David Kulhayne and Jim Houtrides and the rest of the crew from "Sunday Morning". They wanted to interview me. They did and then agreed to do more extensively after the Archbishop's Mass in the morning when I would have more time. They asked if they could film it.

They wanted to center their program around the parish and its people coming back to life. They started to film the people of the wedding rehearsal, as I left. The phone was ringing again and again and again. All the ones trying to reach us for days. One of the first calls was from my classmate Bishop Camacho in Saipan. He said he was fortunate enough to have a redial button. He must have pushed it a hundred times over the two days. He later sent $500.00 to help the people. The Communications Office called. CNN and other media people wanted to film the Mass in the morning. Swell, as long as they're in the side aisle so that they will not distract those who gather to pray.

I had some of the excellent prime rib that the woman cooked. How a good meal can revitalize you! And then off to the shelter with the other priests. More people eating there, less people sleeping there. I went to the area for the sick. The nurses asked me to speak to an elderly couple. She got very upset on seeing me and said I had been neglecting her. One of the priests used to bring Communion to them, and now a lay minister was doing it. She softened as we talked. I ended up visiting them at least twice a day for the four days they were there. The husband was the only one I anointed during the whole time. I delighted in meeting another of our "Communion Call" parishioners. She was reigning like Queen Elizabeth. Her chair was in the center of the corridor. She sat very erect. Her cane was like her scepter. She beamed on all her "subjects", anyone who stopped to talk to her. And it was hard not to stop because she kept saying how good and kind everyone was and how good the food and the care was. It felt good to listen to her positive praise. I stopped a couple times.

Eventually, I got home. I heard a car in the parking lot. It was our music director Steve Meyer. He had driven from Hayward. He had tried to reach me to express concern that he could not reach two of the choir members: Rosalie Cirby and Glen Jones. I was happy to tell him that I had seen both Rosalie and Glen's wife - so all was well. He offered to come for the Archbishop's Mass in the morning. I asked him to stay overnight but he was unprepared to do so. I turned on the TV. Here it was over 48 hours later and only now was I hearing and seeing what happened on the Bay Bridge and I80. I had been living in my own small world which was too big for me. I was exhausted.

And then there was Friday. All the media arrived. All the questions. All the requests. Then the Archbishop arrived with Father Drier. The Archbishop came into the house with me for awhile. I showed him the cracks in the house. I showed him the cracks inside the church tower. He really

wasn't interested. He really had come to see the people and
console them. And that he did. He talked to everyone of them
personally, as he made his way up the aisle to the sacristy.
He chose to wear purple vestments. The three priests of St.
Vincent de Paul concelebrated with him. I proclaimed the
Gospel, quite appropriately, the one for the day was about the
lilies of the field and the birds of the air and God's care
for us. "You have nothing to fear." The Archbishop read a
telegram from the Pope. He preached a moving homily and
composed a spontaneous prayer of the faithful. He forgot no
one. This was his text:

Homily of Archbishop John R. Quinn

In You, O Lord, We Have Hoped

Masses for Earthquake Victims
St. Vincent de Paul Church, San Francisco Marina District, October 20, 1989,
and St. Mary's Cathedral, October 22, 1989

First of all I want to tell you that we have received a message from our Holy Father, Pope John Paul II, which came to me immediately after the earthquake struck. I have not received the actual text in writing because the systems are not working, but I did speak with the representative of the Holy Father, the Papal Nuncio in Washington, and he dictated the message to me over the telephone.

And the message of our Holy Father is this: that he is "deeply saddened by news of the loss of life and the extent of injuries and destruction caused by yesterday's earthquake. The Holy Father commends the victims to Almighty God's eternal love and invokes divine comfort and strength upon individuals and families affected by this immense tragedy. His Holiness joins the population in their suffering and offers special prayers to God for San Francisco and surrounding areas."

Day by day I am communicating with the Papal Nuncio in Washington who informs the Holy Father as things develop with what is happening here. He has asked to be kept informed about what is developing. He is most sincerely mindful of his own visit here in San Francisco and his whole heart is with us in this hour.

I have had the possibility now to visit the shelter at St. Ignatius High School where there are some 200 or more people, I think mostly from the Park Merced area. And I had the opportunity yesterday to visit the shelter here in the Marina and to visit a number of the people and also to visit a number of the parishes and schools, so I can encourage the people in those various places. Today I hope to have the opportunity to visit some of the wounded in the hospitals.

But as I come here this morning I have to confess to you how deeply affected I am by all of this and how helpless I feel. However, I hope and pray that my visit is at least a sign to you of my love and concern and of my desire to stand with you and do something in the face of this suffering which we all experience right now. I am particularly concerned about those elderly people whom I saw yesterday, and I am concerned about the parents and children because I know they must experience fear and anxiety these days and it is so difficult for them. I want you to know that my heart goes out to everyone who is in this situation and that I certainly pray with you to our good God that he will relieve us of this tragedy as soon as possible, and meanwhile give us the courage to endure as long as we must do so.

Now I would like to offer some reflections out of the sources of our faith, the Gospels, that might be a light and a comfort for us in this hour of darkness. I invite you to take an imaginary visit with me to the DeYoung Museum. There are four portraits from the Gospel that I would like you to gaze upon.

The first portrait shows Jesus standing at the grave of his friend Lazarus who had died. And accompanying him are his good friends, Martha and Mary, and some of the apostles and a crowd of other people. The Gospel shows us and this portrait shows us Jesus weeping. It shows us the tenderness and humanness of the heart of Jesus, weeping with his friends in their sorrow and in their loss.

The message of the Gospel is: He is still the same. He is still with his friends. He is now risen from the dead and so he can be with us. And though we do not see him he is still with his friends. He is still with us in the hour of sorrow.

The next portrait I want you to gaze upon is Jesus on the cross. Standing by are the Roman soldiers, the one apostle, Mary his mother and some of the women. In that hour of his suffering and of his mother's suffering—because she was the one who had to stand and watch the one she loved suffer and she could not change that—the portrait shows us Jesus carrying out what the Gospel desribes: "Son, this is your mother. Behold your mother."

For Mary, the Gospel is telling us, is our mother. And with a mother's love she follows everything that happens to us. You know how mothers are; they are concerned about everything that happens to their child, good and bad. The message of the Gospel is that Mary stands—in the hour of the Cross especially—as the mother, stands with the ones she loves, stands with us and is concerned about every aspect of our suffering.

The third portrait is of the upper room where the apostles and disciples are gathered with Mary the mother of the Lord, as the Scripture describes. And through the locked doors comes the risen Jesus. And what is his message to them? Who are these people? They are the apostles, the disciples, they are the ones who abandoned him when he was in his suffering. They had left him and they were frightened. They were confused about what everything meant and what would happen to them and what the future would be. That is as most of us are right now. They were in the same frame of mind.

And what is the first message of Jesus as he enters the room with these confused and frightened and anxious disciples? The first words to them are, "Peace be with you." And then the Scripture says he breathed on them and said, "Receive the Holy Spirit." The Holy Spirit is the one who is the Consoler, who is present in the midst of all our sorrows and all our joys, and whom the risen Christ invites us to turn to in all our sorrows and in all our joys. The Holy Spirit is the Consoler, the one who gives strength, who encourages, who consoles and who heals.

The fourth portrait is not found in the Gospel itself but it reflects everything that the Gospel teaches us. The fourth portrait is of an American priest. He was a chaplain in World War II. At a

A Shepherd's Prayer to
Our Lady of Guadalupe

For His People in a Time of Tragedy

Dearest Mother, Our Lady of Guadalupe, I am shepherd and pastor of this vast people of San Francisco, San Mateo and Marin Counties, the Archdiocese of San Francisco. And today my heart weeps with them and for them. For once more, in this region, we have experienced the tragedy of earthquake.

My heart weeps, dearest Mother, for the old people who are so deeply affected by displacement and so unsettled by the uncertainties of this hour. I weep, too, for the children who are so frightened and filled with anxieties. I weep for the parents who must try to console and reassure them and for the children of the elderly who must sustain and help them in their suffering.

And so I turn to you, dearest Mother, and I place into your hands the suffering and anxieties of this shepherd and all his people. I entrust to you once again all the people whom Christ has placed in my pastoral care. I can never forget that in the hour of His death on the Cross his final valedictory was to give you to us to be our Mother: "Behold your Mother." And so even in this hour of sadness we are filled with hope because you are the bright dawn preparing the noonday splendor of Christ's glory and you are our Mother.

In this difficult hour we turn to you. We pray for the dead and for the bereaved. We pray for the injured. We pray for those who have suffered heavy loss of property and cherished possessions. We pray for the civil authorities, for the public agencies charged with public order and defense of life and property, for the volunteers so generously serving others in need at this time.

But, dearest Mother, we pray with special feeling that you will ask your divine Son, our only Lord, to obtain from the Father that we may be spared any further earthquakes and further disaster. This prayer comes from a shepherd's heart and goes up in complete trust to you. For never was it known that anyone who fled to your protection, implored your help or sought your intercession was left unaided.

May Christ, your son, with the Father and the Holy Spirit, one Lord, one God, hear and answer us that His mercy may be glorified in us and make us rejoice in hope after the scourge of suffering we have endured during these days. Amen.

Archbishop John R. Quinn
October 22, 1989

certain point in the hostilities he was captured by the enemy forces. They tortured him, beat him and left him dying on the floor of the cell. As he lay there dying, having been tortured, all alone, no human support of any kind in the darkness of that cell, in the solitariness of that suffering, he dipped his finger in his own blood and on the wall of that cell he wrote eight Latin words: *"In te Domine speravi, non confundar in aeternum."* Those eight Latin words are from the psalms. They mean, "In you, O Lord, I have hoped, and I will never be disappointed." That is the grace we want now. *In te domine speravi, non confundar in aeternum.* In you, O Lord, I have hoped and I will never be disappointed.

And so we are a people of faith. But we are also a people of hope. "The sufferings of the present time are not worthy to be compared to the glory that is to come." Hope means we have a future. That future is now, even in the midst of tragedy, being prepared by God as the Resurrection was being prepared in the hour of the Cross.

Finally let us take heart from the Word of God, from Psalm 46:

"God is for us a refuge and strength,
A helper close at hand, in time of distress:
So we shall not fear though the earth should rock,
Though the mountains fall into the depths of the sea . . .
The Lord of hosts is with us: the God of Jacob is our stronghold . . .
Be still and know that I am God,
Supreme among the nations, supreme on the earth!
The Lord of hosts is with us. The God of Jacob is our stronghold." □

After Mass, again he was one with the people - the warmest I've seen him.

And then he was off and I was being interviewed again for TV. I must have been boring because none of my half hour of brilliance ever made the screen, only my proclaiming the Gospel.

I was anxious to get back to the Marina. Many of our good parishioners I had not seen since the quake. I went through those streets where the only activity was construction by PG&E crews or destruction by wrecking companies. I knocked on doors. I talked to neighbors. I found that most of the ones I was looking for had moved to children's homes. One person I looked for lived on Beach. I went through the barriers on Divisadero and Cervantes - at the pile of rubble that had once been an apartment building owned by old parishioners and where many of our families lived; no one was on those blocks of Divisadero. Except for a few PG&E men at the corner, the same was true on Beach. It was a deserted city. The man I was looking for had just gotten out of the hospital. He lived alone. He was not home. I was worried. I walked back to the corner, and there he was, the only figure on the street slowly walking toward me carrying a plastic bag with a quart of milk and a paper. Even without water and electricity and gas, he wasn't about to abandon his home. He said that he just went to bed earlier than before.

When I got back to the rectory, I immediately got a phone call from a polite but angry and determined young man. His sister-in-law had burned to death in the fire at 3701 Divisadero. Her name was Janet Brown Ray. She and her husband had been trapped. He freed himself but could not free her. She insisted that he flee the flames and live and tell her family of her belief in God and her love for them. The family wanted a service at the site of her death. They had asked everyone for permission to enter the area to do this. All the bureaucratic doors were closed. It was too dangerous. There was no way. They were angry. I was their last resort, as the local pastor. I said I would try. I decided not to work uphill. I started at the top. I called the mayor's office. I explained the circumstances to the secretary. She referred me to a man in Assemblywoman Jackie Speier's office. He listened and was kind and gave me four numbers through which I could try to reach the Chief of Police who would have to approve. The first number was constantly busy. The second one was answered immediately by a Myrna Snider. She listened

and said she would try to get the necessary permission. I
phoned the family in Lafayette to tell of my progress. They
said that they would leave immediately, in the hope the
permission would be given. An hour later, I received a call
saying it would be okay, how many would be with me (I guessed
three or four), what time tomorrow would be best. I said they
were on their way; they wanted it today. More contacts, but
before the family arrived at St. Vincent de Paul everything
was arranged. We walked down to the Marina Middle School -
all twelve of us! She had sisters and brothers and their
spouses and children as well as parents. They carried roses.
I suggested they not display them, if they wished to avoid the
spotlight of the press; they hid them in a coat. Captain
Martell and another officer asked how many were going in: I
started to count the family one by one. They got the point
and provided two police cars with flashing red lights.
Slowly, we were driven through the rubble. We parked by the
Newcomer School and walked to the site. The only ones around
were reporters and photographers. They sensed what was
occurring and very kindly respected the sorrow and the privacy
of the family. I could see them slowly move back against the
nearby homes, the only sign of their presence was the
occasional click of a camera. It was silent. When I was not
praying aloud, all that could be heard was the water of the
bay from blocks away and the crackling of the still smoldering
fire in front of us. We prayed. We wept. Each of them threw
a rose on the site of her death. The police led us through
the people that had gathered at the corner. I spotted one of
our diocesan priests, he was dressed as a policeman! A woman
came running to me. She was Alicia Yabar our cook on Mondays.
She lived in the building that almost caught fire on Beach.
She was staying with her family. I asked her to phone so we
could help. The press did not bother us. The police drove
us back to St. Vincent de Paul. A family I hadn't heard of
four hours before, I had now become a part of through grief
and sympathy. They asked if they could set up a Memorial Fund
to aid others through St. Vincent de Paul Church. They asked
me to administer it. In the coming month 115 gifts were
received. $7,243.00 was donated to help other families hurt
by the earthquake.

A dinner of cold turkey and back with the other priests
to the Marina Middle School. More and more of the local
residents were appearing to share in the excellent meals that
were being offered, but less and less of the local people were
staying for the night, only a few who had no local family and
were afraid to be alone at night. I continued to be amazed
at the friendliness and kindness of all the volunteers, the
vast majority of them in their twenties and thirties. One of
the many that I congratulated on their goodness whispered to

me that he was a former priest from Portland. I was pleased
to see kids from our school volunteering: David in the kitchen
and Eric setting up cots plus some of the high school students
in the cafeteria serving others.

Saturday was a day preparing for Sunday, seeing that the
church was thoroughly cleaned for the people. And there was
the wedding. With lights and organ and all the frills as if
this was just an ordinary week. And then there was time to
finish preparing a homily. I had much to say. One of the
topics demanded consultation immediately by phone with all who
had been working with me on a million dollar Endowment Fund
Drive for St. Vincent de Paul School. It was supposed to be
in high gear when the quake hit. Potential major donors had
been informed of it. All school parents had been contacted
by mail and by phone. All Sunday envelope users had received
literature in the mail, some of them had been called. The
mailing was almost ready to go to all the other parishioners.
Those who had worked hard in the preparations agreed with me
so I added the topic to my list of points for Sunday and wrote
the following letter to all parishioners.

The Church of
St. Vincent de Paul
2320 Green Street
San Francisco, California
94123-4625

October 23, 1989

Dear Parishioners:

I apologize for sending you so many letters. When the first was written, little did I know that a second and a third would be necessary.

On October 1st, I preached on the St. Vincent de Paul School Endowment Fund and stated that raising a million dollars for such a fund was necessary for the continual excellence and existence of our school. I begged for you to give this fund highest priority in your generosity.

I know that this Fund is still necessary, but I also know that it would be insensitive of me to ask you to give it such priority in the light of the earthquake. There are human needs in your lives or those of your neighbors that demand that priority and your charity.

With this letter I am, therefore, suspending this Endowment Fund Drive. We will not refuse any gifts that are freely given, but we will not as of this date solicit any future donations. We will contact all who have already made donations and ascertain their will as to what they have so generously and quickly given.

Let us pray that God in His goodness will help you to meet your own needs and those of your neighbors now - and that He, one day, in less stressful times and in His own mysterious way will help us to provide financial stability for our parish school so that it will continue in existence and in excellence for all the generations yet to come.

May God grant you comfort and hope in these stress-filled days.

Yours in Christ, -

Reverend John Kevin Ring
Pastor

JKR:cm

It is a great set-back for the school, but there was nothing else I could do without being insensitive to the people.

An hour before the evening Mass, the PG&E arrived to light the pilot lights. Again, we could cook and we'd have hot water.

On Saturday night, Mrs. Matteucci had the three of us priests to her place for dinner. It was the first good one that we had enjoyed since Monday. We needed it. Even there, I got a call from the rectory. CBS wanted to hear from me as soon as possible. They wanted to film my Mass on Sunday and in particular my sermon. Swell.

The three of us went to visit the people at the shelter. I was happy to see that many more were gone, some to St. Anne's Home, others to Mercy Retirement Center. Among the ones to St. Anne's were the man I had anointed and his wife who was annoyed with me the first night. We had become friends again. In the cafeteria, I went from table to table talking to the people. One of the young volunteers said that she noted that one old man seemed to enjoy talking to me. Would I go back and try to encourage him to move to the shelter. He was hiding in his apartment and it was red-tagged. I did. He was a former seaman and reformed alcoholic. Rather crusty. One of my persuasive arguments was that he'd be able to shower. I said that was something I was looking forward to tonight. The gas had just been turned on so I'd be having my first hot shower in five days. He smiled at me and said: "I was going to say something to you Father, but I thought I'd offend you!" Laughter but a lost argument. I saw him later that night being interviewed on TV - his little knit cap on his head and a twinkle in his eye as he spoke of being from New York but having his heart in San Francisco.

It was good to see the people at Sunday Mass, like a reunion. Not as many as last week, infact down about a sixth in attendance. I preached at all the Masses this sermon and gave these announcements and prayers:

SERMON

"Come to me" Jesus has said to us during these days - and we have come to Him in prayer often as individuals and as families within our homes and on our streets, in our shelters and in our church. Come to me - and as the Parish Community of St. Vincent de Paul - we have come together in prayer today - prayers of gratitude by those who survived, prayers of sorrow for those who died, prayers of petition for those in need, prayers of thanksgiving for all the good people who came to help us in our need.

Come to me - and we have come - to be honest to our God and say that in the past five days we have not found his yoke to be easy and his burden to be light. The earth shook and we shook; our homes were shaken and some of them fell and we were shaken and our spirits fell. For some, possessions were lost forever; for others, they were chipped and scarred. But how little when we think of those who lost relatives and friends and neighbors. Yes, a yoke that was not easy, a burden that was not light.

And so we have come to be honest before God and say that we have found life burdensome this week and that we are weary and that we need him. We need Him to refresh us. We need Him to strengthen us. We need Him to comfort us. We need Him to console us. We need Him to enlighten and enliven us. We need this of Him who is gentle and humble of heart.

And slowly He has or slowly He will enlighten and enliven us. He will enliven us by giving us a new and profound appreciation of our life and by helping us to strip away what is useless or distracting and by helping us to come to a new and enriched sense of values. And He will enlighten us to see that alone, in an earthquake and even without one, alone we are helpless. At all times we need Him and we need one another.

How I have been enlightened by Him in these days through the immediate prayer that I'm sure we all said at the first shock, through being able to fall on my knees here before the altar moments after, in fear and in humility and in prayers of petition for you and all who I love, here gazing at Him on the cross, suffering alone, abandoned, nailed to the cross, in his suffering so he could not run. And for him an earthquake offered not just the possibility, it was a sign of His death. And then I was enlightened to see that I could not be alone, as a priest, as your pastor, as well as a person, I had to be with others. I had to be with you. And how I found Him in you as immediately after I found you on your streets and in your homes, in the shelter and here at church. How beautiful to see that fear was becoming faith and despair was becoming prayer, suffering was turning to acceptance, need was turning to hope, and weakness becoming strength, and uncertainty was becoming courage, and strangers were becoming friends. The worst in the earth's nature was bringing out the best in human nature. The worst moments in our lives were bringing out the goodness within our hearts. What was separating the layers of the earth was uniting the people of the earth. Out of evil God was bringing to birth the goodness and holiness we too often hide. Like the early Christians, it could be said of the people of the Marina: See how they love one another. I was proud to be with you - I was proud to be your Pastor.

Proud to see you consoling neighbors on their losses, welcoming strangers into your homes, giving comfort to the elderly, wiping away the tears of children, guiding the confused to the shelter, feeding the hungry, and giving drink to the thirsty.

How beautiful to see the response of the fire and police and water and medical departments, and the PG&E and telephone companies and all who provided food and bedding and clothing. In particular the work of the Red Cross, I cannot praise them enough. (In fact the second collection today - except what is clearly designated for the Propagation of the Faith will be for the local chapter of the Red Cross who served this community so lovingly and cheerfully.) And how grateful I was to Archbishop Quinn who with Bishop Sevilla came over as soon as they could to visit us and see the parish and then returned to visit the shelter and on Friday to offer Mass here at St. Vincent de Paul for those who died and those who survived.

And then there were the young people, God bless them, the ones in their 20's and 30's, all those beautiful young people that I saw by day and night at the Marina Middle School. All volunteers guiding, directing, comforting, curing, serving, cleaning, cheering, caring. As I said to some of the elderly they were protecting: so good and so beautiful that you'd love to take them home with you - real grandchildren could not be more loving. (I'd ordain them all as priests tomorrow. They'd save this world in no time by their spirit and their joy.)

St. Vincent de Paul's was known as the Church of the Exposition. The upper part of our edifice was finished in order to serve the 1915 Panama Pacific Exposition in the Marina. As the Marina will now rise again, may we the people of today be the Exposition, the ones who expose and show forth the faith and hope and love that our world so desperately needs. As the lower part of this edifice, as well as the rectory, survived the '06 earthquake and served as a place for people to worship as well as to serve people as a food distribution center. So may St. Vincent de Paul today be a place for you to worship and from which you can go forth to serve the needs of others with love and joy with which we are being enlightened and enlivened during these days.

1) Second collection - for the Red Cross except for the envelopes clearly designated for the Propagation of the Faith as had been announced. ($5,041.00 was given to the Red Cross through this collection. As noted earlier, the Janet Ray Brown Fund raised $7,243.00. In addition to this, $18,205.00 was given to the parish. All of this was given to people in need within the parish.)

2) For any who wish to come and talk and pray about the events of these days, the priests of our parish will be available here in the church on Monday at 1:00 p.m. and at 7:00 p.m. and, as with the other priests, I'll be available at other times by appointment.

3) For donations of clothing or food, call Red Cross or Salvation Army.

4) For school students - on Monday, school will reopen if okayed by the Fire Department. The structure is okay. Though there is a considerably large amount of plaster that must be replaced at the Christmas break. Only the alarm system must be checked out now.

5) As for the church, the angels by the altar are a bit tipsy, but the foundations are strong - the cracks will have to be studied further - stations were at varying angles - over 100 lbs. of plaster each - so removed forever - for your safety. (It was later discovered that the crosses on the church roof had twisted and split their seams. Three had to be removed).

6) We have had calls from your friends across the city and nation. They know this is your church and ask about you. If you are at a temporary phone or dwelling leave your name and phone number or address at the rectory and we will tell them when they call.

7) As for the million dollar Endowment Fund Drive for our school, as much as we need major donations, we feel your needs have highest priority. We won't refuse donations, but we won't seek any. God will provide.

PRAYERS OF THE FAITHFUL

For all who have been affected by this earthquake in our community and in others that we continue to be people of faith and of hope and of love,

(let us pray to the Lord)

For all the volunteers and all those whose work brought them to the service of this community, that they continue to be in less stressful days the people of love and of joy that they have been for us during these sad days,

(let us pray to the Lord)

For all who have died in this earthquake and all who survived it, that they know the peace of Christ and the consolation of the Spirit,

(let us pray to the Lord)

At the 10:00 a.m. Mass, CBS was supposed to be filming. No sign of them. I was relieved. As I was leaving the pulpit, however, I spotted them up in the choir loft. I heard later that on the evening news, they showed me as I preached and as I greeted the people outside - but it was Tom Brokaw who was doing the speaking. They used my body and his words!

It is too bad that they didn't show the conclusion of my sermon; one of the little children broke away from his family and ran up the side aisle and across the front and down the center, followed by his sister whom he kept eluding and then his embarrassed mother. His athletic father stayed in the pew. It was a source of good healthy laughter for all, a good remedy, but I told the people I was actually finished talking anyway so it was no solution for future Sundays if I talked too long. All of the Liturgies were enhanced by the well-chosen hymns "O God Our Help In Ages Past", "On Eagles' Wings" and "A Mighty Fortress Is Our God." The Psalm for the Sunday could not have been more appropriate - Psalm 121 on how the Lord guards us. The prayerfulness of the people was evident. Their joy at seeing one another was obvious.

Monday saw the reopening of the parish school. Classroom discussions and opportunities to express verbally and visually what they experienced were good therapy for the children. A number of them were alone at the time. Some were trapped in their buildings. One saw her home burn. Others saw their buildings collapse. Many were on the Marina Green for soccer practice and saw the earth move in waves in front of them. We concluded the school day with a Mass. The normally quiet children were quite jittery. No wonder! How good they are. In the Prayers of the Faithful, they did not pray only for themselves. They prayed also for the people of Japan who suffered from an earthquake earlier that day.

The following day marked the one-week anniversary of the earthquake of '89. Sensing that people would be remembering that fact and be outside, I spent the greater part of the afternoon walking through the Marina. I talked to PG&E men about their progress. I stopped at the Marina Middle School to ascertain the current situation. As I walked from block to block, I talked to people still uncertain as to their future. I talked to children who showed me where they were. I talked one girl into entering her home for the first time. She had been staying with a girlfriend out of the area. I entered with her and blessed the home and the family and prayed for the safety of all the area and the parish.

It was Tuesday 5:04 p.m. again. In the midst of fallen and cracked buildings, I was talking to a man whose grief-filled face was in the paper the morning after. His face was still grief-filled.

I started to walk back toward the church. I met one of the young adults of the parish. He was watering the plants outside his damaged home. He said that, even if he couldn't live there because of the damage, the plants could but they needed water in order to be alive when he was able to return. I met a little old Italian woman. She too had returned for 5:04 p.m. Her home was tilting. Her driveway was topsy-turvy. And there she was with her broom sweeping the dirt and the debris into the cracks in her sidewalk. Her house would be neat when she returned.

It had been but a week, and what a week it was. But already sidewalks were being swept and plants watered and people were planning to return. The earth had quaked but the people of the Marina and the people of St. Vincent de Paul were still alive. A little shaken, but a better community, a more concerned Church for all we had endured together. The quake of '89 and the role of each one of us was now history.